Special Forces Interpreter

Special Forces Interpreter

An Afghan on Operations with the Coalition

Eddie Idrees

Pen & Sword
MILITARY

First published in Great Britain in 2021 by
Pen & Sword Military
An imprint of
Pen & Sword Books Ltd
Yorkshire – Philadelphia

ISBN 978 1 52675 850 7

Typeset by Mac Style
Printed and bound in the UK by CPI Group (UK) Ltd,
Croydon, CR0 4YY.

Pen & Sword Books Limited incorporates the imprints of Atlas,
Archaeology, Aviation, Discovery, Family History, Fiction, History,
Maritime, Military, Military Classics, Politics, Select, Transport,
True Crime, Air World, Frontline Publishing, Leo Cooper, Remember
When, Seaforth Publishing, The Praetorian Press, Wharncliffe
Local History, Wharncliffe Transport, Wharncliffe True Crime
and White Owl.

For a complete list of Pen & Sword titles please contact

PEN & SWORD BOOKS LIMITED
47 Church Street, Barnsley, South Yorkshire, S70 2AS, England
E-mail: enquiries@pen-and-sword.co.uk
Website: www.pen-and-sword.co.uk

Or

PEN AND SWORD BOOKS
1950 Lawrence Rd, Havertown, PA 19083, USA
E-mail: Uspen-and-sword@casematepublishers.com
Website: www.penandswordbooks.com

Contents

About the Author

Eddie Idrees was born in Kabul in 1985. His father was a colonel in the Afghan army and his mother was a university lecturer. In the early 1990s he went into exile with his family in Pakistan. They returned after the defeat of the Taliban in 2002.

From 2004 to 2007, Eddie worked as an interpreter for US special forces and in 2007 became an interpreter at the Counter Insurgency Academy in Kabul. In 2009 he became an interpreter for the British army's elite regiment, the SAS, and was decorated for his war work. He has taken part in over 500 Special Operations.

After he and his family suffered credible death threats, he left Afghanistan in 2012 and moved to Britain, where he has performed a number of jobs, including working for an agricultural company, and interpreting for local councils, the NHS and within the criminal justice system. He now combines studying psychology at a British university, where he has completed his Undergraduate and MA qualifications, with working for an organization operating in Europe.

Eddie Idrees is a pseudonym.

Acknowledgements

I would like to dedicate this book to all the 'Unknown heroes' of Afghanistan. They were hired as interpreters, but they carried out the role of an army, police and advisors who saved many innocent civilian lives whilst fighting the war on terror and sacrificing their lives in the process. With one goal in mind, to have a better Afghanistan. To the over 2000 interpreters who lost their lives in this war, yet none was recognized by any party. I would also thank those who helped in the ways they could, in particular Deborah Haynes and other journalist who made the voice of Interpreters heard in the UK.

Prologue

I owe this country nothing. I have fought for her, and she has fed and sheltered me. Better, she has given me opportunity. She is not my country, but I love what she stands for. My country, which I love, does not love me, nor does it love what I wish it had, which is what this country has. I owe my own country nothing. I have fought for her, and she has spurned me. I love her but she has exiled me, and scattered my family across the world. Despite this, I love her.

I was born in war, and have known war all my life. But now I live in peace in a land of peace. To be more precise, at this exact moment I am sitting peacefully with my would-be brothers in a café. These brothers, who live in peace, in a land of peace and have never known war, talk of nothing but.

I don't quite remember how I came here, except that I met these guys at a friend's shop in London and somehow we adopted this run-down café nearby. I think my current bout of homesickness was brought on by the presence of two Afghan 'brothers'. I must stop doing this.

Apart from my two compatriots, I cannot remember the nationalities of the others in this ad-hoc debating group. Is there a Tunisian? An Iraqi? I am pretty sure there's a Bangladeshi. They have all been eclipsed in my memory by the shining moon-face fringed with an orange beard that holds forth in a soft Irish accent.

He speaks with the joy and intensity of the convert. The others look a bit shifty. Converts are always a bit embarrassing. They call each other 'brother' and 'sister' rather too often, keen to try out all the new forms of language they have recently learned, all at once and at every opportunity. They are mostly romanticizing some ideology which is unacceptable to many in Muslim countries, but they have a different understanding of those countries; they see these backward, ignorant Muslims around them as true representatives of the people in those countries.

Michael, now Mohammed, is in full flow on the subject of the hour. Discovering that I am an Afghan, especially one just arrived from Afghanistan, he is delighted at the chance to commune with another of the world's most oppressed peoples, hinting at the depth of his own people's persecution to emphasise our brotherhood.

He warms to his theme, exhorting me to return home to fight for the Taliban and liberate my country from the infidel. The other two Afghans are looking really uncomfortable now. They have undoubtedly recognised me as being of Tajik background, and are therefore very unlikely to be fans of the Taliban. In fact I can see that they are already having second thoughts about welcoming me into their group. They mumble agreement with the Irish man. I pay them no mind: my own cousins are just as bad. I recently had a blazing row with some of them who had fled the war fifteen years ago to come to Britain. They whined on about how things were better under the Taliban, and how a woman's honour was safer. *Safer*! Women across Afghanistan are persecuted and punished and abused!

As the Irishman chides me for dodging jihad, I realise how much I miss my war, and wish I was back in it. This is not because of the remote theoretical chance that I might kill this Irish idiot.

I miss the war every day. I miss the war because we made a difference. I miss the feeling of waiting at the pan for the CH47s, the walk towards the Chinook, hearing the beautiful noise of its engines. I miss taking off and seeing the lights of the camp lying below us, receding as the Chinook manoeuvres away from the camp. I miss seeing dead Taliban. I miss being with the SAS: that feeling of being invincible alongside the best in the world!

Perhaps the Irishman also misses war, now that his own country is at peace. Perhaps that is why he converted, on the enemy's enemy principle. I should not grudge him his armchair belligerence. Perhaps one day he too will make the journey to war: in Syria or Iraq, Somalia or even Afghanistan, or on some as-yet-unopened front. Or perhaps his enthusiasm will drive him to atomise himself in some shopping mall or terminus. Back on his native island in some drizzly suburb, his astonished neighbours will say, 'he seemed such a quiet lad, always reading his books.'

I owe this country nothing, but the same war I fought in Afghanistan against ignorance, prejudice and evil has insinuated itself here in Britain. I do my best. I tell recently-arrived immigrants not to send their youngsters to the local mosque. I tell them to give them a choice, and they nearly all make the choice not to go to the mosque. After all, they didn't struggle across thousands of miles only to be told what to do by another idiot with a beard. I do my best, but my fighting days have been curtailed.

Overview

S*pecial Forces Interpreter* is the story of my life so far. I was one of the top interpreters for the British army in Afghanistan. I went on over 500 special operations with US Forces and the SAS and was senior interpreter at the Counter Insurgency Academy in Kabul (COIN). My father was a colonel in the Afghan army, and I was born into war. It is no exaggeration to say that I have spent my whole life under the threat of death from religious, tribal and political factions in my home country.

What I didn't realise was that the war I was born into had spilled out of my home and was being waged around the world, in Iraq and Syria and Turkey, Pakistan and India, and on the streets of Europe. There is jihad in the Sahel and assaults by Somalians – led by British women – in African shopping malls. Some of the wellsprings of terror are found on the housing estates of Britain. And all the while in Afghanistan the long war against the Taliban goes on. The war I was born into is the same war my father fought – the war against blind tradition and religious ignorance. Ultimately it is a battle to bring Afghanistan into the modern world, and to retain its integrity as a state. It is a conflict that has scattered my family to the four corners of the world and forced me to flee to the UK under threat of death from the corrupt Afghan establishment in Kabul – and the Taliban.

My war has shaped me and helped me to understand the underlying reasons for this pandemic of religious violence.

Little did I realise that when I came to Britain my war would come with me. I feel its presence in two ways. First, I have had to recognise and confront the post-traumatic stress disorder that I have brought with me. Secondly, in Britain, which I believed to be a rational country, I have found a deep and dark well of ignorance among Afghan and other immigrants, in particular the Muslim, Asian community, and a wilful blindness to it among the broader British population.

These are new battles, for me personally, and for my adopted country.

Chapter 1

Dreams and Reality

As children, we all dream of achieving things. For some it is about money, for some it is about becoming someone. Others believe in a cause, a cause developed because of experiences or images we saw during our childhood. For me, I had a dream, a dream of becoming someone, from seeing the image of my father, the uniform he wore, and knowing the reason he wore it. I always dreamed of becoming a solider, like my father who served for over three decades in the Afghan army, an honest officer, a great father, a loyal husband. Not only was he a kind father, but he remains to this day the wisest man I have ever met, someone from whom I learned much during my childhood. His evening stories after dinner taught us so many life lessons. A few of my siblings did not like his stories, but I always enjoyed listening to him, not only for his experiences and the operations he conducted during his service, but also because, as I today understand, he aimed to teach us life lessons and be prepared for the challenges I have been facing all my life. But life doesn't go as we dream or expect. We only learn about our strengths and weaknesses as we live, our capabilities and our limitations, and we encounter unforeseen obstacles.

I have taken part in many special operations in my life. I have seen hundreds of terrorists getting killed, killed in so many ways. Some shot in the body, bombed (which means they were in pieces, literally!), shot in the eyes, shot in the head with brains all over the ground. I couldn't count the number of ways we killed these terrorists. I never felt anything for the terrorist Taliban, never felt bad for them. The only ones I felt bad for were the kids. Children are innocent, no matter what their fathers or mothers do; there is no children-terrorist in my eyes, and they are one of the biggest victims of the forty plus years of war in Afghanistan.

The cold air was completely still. No doubt the stars twinkled brightly above but I was in the green world of my night-vision goggles. At last after our six-kilometre march, through typical rugged, mountainous Afghan terrain, we were at the compound. It was a world at peace, or at least fast asleep, and dark – electricity is a foreign concept in that region. Four of us were to go up, and we silently got our ladders ready and approached the rough mud brick wall that loomed above us. It was about ten feet high. The rest of the team deployed to surround the compound.

After laying the ladders carefully against the wall we ascended silently, like ghosts. Or rather my SAS comrades were like ghosts. I shouldn't think they made a single noise as they climbed. I did my best, which wasn't bad I think, and we took position perching on our ladders, looking down into the courtyard of the compound and onto the dwelling running along one side of it. Now it was time for my sweaty-bollock moment. It is a cliché to say that adrenalin pumps through you, but it does. I was in a state of hyper-alertness. I was honed. I was ready. This is what I do. I wanted the innocent to remain unharmed and the guilty to be punished.

'Come out unarmed with your hands up! You are surrounded! Leave your weapons inside and come out! Women, children and men!' I shouted.

There was no movement, but I felt very exposed. Even though it was a moonless night we were outlined against the stars, and of course I was the one opening my yap. I reiterated my request, and we heard movement. The building was stirring. No lights were showing, but there was the muffled sound of people moving around, and voices.

'Come out unarmed, with your hands up! You are surrounded! Do not think you can avoid being killed if you come out armed!'

The three snipers with me on the wall were aiming at the door of the building as it slowly opened. One dim figure came out, then another, then another. Or rather they must have seemed dim to each other, but to us with our goggles the scene was nearly pin sharp. What I saw stunned me. The lead terrorist was holding up a little girl in front of him. He was clearly armed and had his chest webbing on. He thought we could not see his weapon and ammunition – I guess he thought we could see only as much as he could in the dark. The two others were also armed. I froze. I could see the snipers' dots on the terrorist's head, just above the sleepy, squirming figure of the child.

'Put her down! Put her down! Drop your weapons!' I shouted, fearing that the child might get hurt.

He lifted her up and turned around towards me, where the voice was coming from. He obviously couldn't see the dots on his head, or if he knew they were there, he believed he held the ace.

It happened very quickly and very slowly at the same time. The snipers shot him. I was staring at the girl as she fell with her father. How did I know she was his daughter? I didn't. Instinct perhaps, but I was subsequently proved right. She was covered in blood. We had shot her. I don't think I noticed the other two men being shot – it was probably practically simultaneous with their child-toting comrade – as I was fixated on the figure of the little girl. She was moving just a little as she lay half under the lifeless body of her father.

My mind was giving commands that my body couldn't obey fast enough, like I was swimming in treacle. A screaming fear and a rising anger was boiling within me. I slipped over the wall and dropped into the compound. I ran towards the child, turning on my torch and ripping off my night goggles. The three men of the sniper team dropped behind me into the compound. They had had no choice once I had gone in. I heard a muttered, 'Fuck's sakes Eddie!' I had ignored all procedure; I was putting us all in danger. But I didn't care. I could only think of the little girl.

And more than the little girl. Images swirled into my mind as if I was drowning. The starving kids by the road who had greeted me off the bus to Kabul. Me and my cousin being rounded up to be beaten in the mosque. All of the kids trodden underfoot by the Taliban. All the kids whose future they betrayed. I was freaking out, but I moved quickly as I rolled the body of her father over and pulled the girl towards me. All those kids. The execution at the football match. Everything. Everything that had made me hate the Taliban. All the innocent Afghans killed, killed in maternity wards, at schools, at universities, or in their homes. All those Afghan women abused and raped, all the child marriages and forced marriages, selling women like pieces of property, treating children like slaves. All was summed up in one shining point in my mind. How could he do this? He had sacrificed his own daughter. How old was she? About three? About the same age as my daughter. Fathers are supposed to protect their children, to die protecting them, not to sacrifice them for their own selfishness. But these terrorists have no mercy killing others: kids, women, or other innocent men.

My hands moved quickly over her face to clear the blood. She squirmed and cried. Thank God, she was alive. Then she began to cry, calling for her father and mother. I was on my knees in a world of my own at the time, I had no idea what was going on around me. Where was I? There was no awareness of my location, the situation. I wiped away the slimy mess from her head and hair. There was no sign of wounds on her head. But where was the blood coming from? I had to check. My hands were on autopilot, instinct and training kicking in I suppose, but my mind was filled with emotion.

I was furious but lurking underneath was the chilling thought that we might have shot her. Us. That it was a British bullet in her. The smell of blood reeked in my nostrils, over and above the usual dried cow-shit smell of the yard.

I tried to take her clothes off to check the rest of her body. But now she was squirming away from my grasp screaming, 'No! No!' The harder I tried to undress her, the harder she wriggled and cried. She might have been only three but her father had probably already told her it was a sin to show her body to a man. And now she was going to die because of it, bleeding to death from the wound under her clothes.

Suddenly I had an idea. I picked her up and ran through the door of the compound to the outside. We had a female medic. In fact we had a couple of women soldiers with us. I shouted for her as I ran out. 'Medic! Medic! Medic!!'

The medic came straight away.

'I think she's been hit! Check her and see if she is shot! She won't let me!'

I handed the wriggling bundle over to the medic who knelt down with her, placing her gently on the ground. The medic was also worried, but she was calmer than I was. She started to undo her clothing. The little girl screamed and tried to crawl away.

'Take your helmet off,' I shouted to the medic. 'She thinks you're a man.' I told the medic, if you show that you are a female, she will be more comfortable.

The medic took off her helmet and pulled her hair down, shaking it at the girl and making soothing noises. The girl calmed down. The kid realised that it was a woman in uniform and she felt at ease. I stepped away as she let the medic loosen her clothes and check her for wounds.

After a few stressful minutes: 'She's okay,' said the medic. 'She's unhurt.'

I very much doubted that. She had lost her father. I started to calm down. It wasn't really a feeling of relief – I just had to get on with my job. I went back into the compound rooms. The medic followed me carrying the child. In the yard, women and children had now appeared. Some of them were silent. Some were crying seeing the bodies of their men on the floor.

'Eddie?' said the sergeant major.

'Yeah, sure,' I replied and went to talk to the women. I resumed my job by questioning everyone in the house to get as much information as possible. But first I had to calm them down, and I had to make sure they would stay in one room until we had completed our operation.

Insurgents all over Afghanistan, and in particular in the south, had a fear of night operations. One of their names for us was 'the night raiders' – probably because our operations were mostly violent raids in the night. Other names were the bearded devils, and the green-eyed devils (which was my favourite), and so on. I would listen to their chit-chat on their radios. They were so scared that they would shit themselves when they heard our helicopters coming in, or any helicopter at night. Terrorists were going to die that night.

What I loved about our operations was that we didn't go after 'ten dollar' Taliban, we went after their leadership and hardcore Taliban, or those who were an immediate threat to the Afghan public. They would not surrender, and the SAS did not lose or give up, so most of our operations ended in killing them. This was pleasing: the more terrorists killed, the less there were to kill innocent Afghans around the country.

Chapter 2

Exile in Pakistan – *Panahendagee dar Pakistan*

To be a refugee is to be at the bottom of every pile. You are a nuisance to everyone, except when you can be exploited. Nobody wants to hear the story of your previous life. In fact, the better it was, the more you are despised. You are nothing. No wonder the Taliban found the camps such a rich recruiting ground.

My father spurned the refugee camps with their febrile and violent communities, and found us a house in Peshawar. Most of the camps contained extremists. My father did not want us to become extremists. He wanted his sons and daughters to have opportunities. He wanted us to live in a better community, to have a roof over our heads, and to have enough food.

From being a high-ranking Afghan officer he went from door to door looking for work. He became an unemployed refugee – a third-class citizen. No job was too humiliating – he would often work as a servant to the most appalling people. Some couldn't even read. When my father was an officer, our house butler was more educated than these people. Occasionally he was a driver. More often than not he worked as a cleaner. He was mocked and despised, but he never lost heart and I never once remember him complaining. He kept our home, and though not comfortable, we never went without food. He was under much stress, but his smile was always there and his advice never changed.

I went to school with my brother. After a couple of fights we learned not to talk about politics. The school was full of refugees, who were fixated by what was happening in their country. No matter what the age of the students, politics was the hot topic. That was our game, our country was the playground now. The Afghans were not the only ones with strong views on Afghan politics: the Pakistanis were also obsessed with it, and not in any way that I could agree with. They were for Hekmatyar at that time, so I kept my mouth shut, and learned to control my temper.

There were two benefits of exile though. The first would transform my life in a way I could not have imagined at the time. I learned English in Peshawar. I had a wonderful teacher, who loved his subject, and could convey something of the beauty of the language and the world that created it even during the driest of grammar lessons.

Our school was in an area called Saddere in Peshawar. It was an Afghan school funded by the United Nations for the Afghan refugees. The funding to Afghan schools was limited, so there were basically no facilities in Afghan schools. No chair or desks, it was just a house with three to four bedrooms, and most of the classes were in tents on the roof, hallways or yards. Tents were aid from the United Nations for refugees. I still remember the blue tents with UNHCR written on them. The only office in the school was the principal's – small, one window, three or four chairs and a desk. Of course, due to lack of funding, there was no library at the school. Afghan schools for refugees were registered with the Pakistani government, yet independent in what they taught. It was more like a private school. It had no heating, so was really cold during winters; all students had to wear a few layers to keep warm. There were around 150 pupils, a primary, secondary and high school all together. Due to the low number of students it was a mixed-sex school, but even though we had girls as our class mates, it was forbidden to talk to them. Mainly it was a rule set up by our extremist principal, a pro-Taliban, an extremely ignorant principal. One day I was wearing a T-shirt and he, for some reason, thought that showing your arms to a boy was offensive. That day I was asked to go to the principal's office, and, after a lengthy and boring lecture on Islam and Afghan culture, he punished me by beating me with a stick. The way Afghan teachers punish students is to hit them with a stick or cable on the palm or back of the hands. If it is a stick, the beating keeps going until the stick is broken, no matter how much you suffer or cry. We just hoped the stick would break before we did.

Even though our principal was a lunatic extremist Taliban, the rest of our teachers were absolutely brilliant! In particular, two of my female teachers, who were very kind and well educated. One of them not only opposed the rule to not speak to the opposite sex, but she actually created opportunities for us to engage in classrooms. Of course she would always keep an eye out for the principal, and when he was around she would let us know.

Luckily for us, the principal was not a teacher. He was either sitting in his office or annoying students by lecturing us on religion and how the Taliban were 'great'. We could not have opposed this man, so no matter what he said we had to keep quiet, pretend we were listening and just nod! Every morning, before entering our classrooms, he would make us sing songs, with no music. They were all songs for Afghanistan, and whoever was singing the 'Taliban' song, that student would become his favorite, and at the end he would tell them, God bless them and their future is bright.

Most of our teachers were female. The pay teachers received was not enough to feed a family, so the men looked for other jobs. I am glad we had Afghan women as teachers: they were intelligent, kind, their method was easy to understand, and, importantly, they focused on what mattered and taught us only about religion when the subject was religion. In Afghan schools we had more than twelve subjects: languages, such as Dari literature, Pashtu and English literature, religious subjects, such as Quran, Hadith and other interpretations of Islam, sports, history, physics, biology, Sharia law, algebra, craft, chemistry (a subject that I disliked), poetry and many more.

Unlike in Afghanistan, schools in Pakistan were not free; you had to pay a fee. So my father had to work extra hard to pay for all of us to go to school.

The United Nations used to provide limited stationery and other school books for the students. Unfortunately the school principal would only give these books to his chosen students. The stationery he sold to shops or to parents for a discounted price.

In spite of all the financial difficulties, and the extremist ideology of the principal, I enjoyed learning. I was not very interested in the religious topics, but I was in love with history, geography, poetry and English literature. In the back of my mind however, I always wanted to do what my father did: to become a soldier and serve my country, Afghanistan.

My father used to tell me his life story, how he was an obedient child and how that attitude got him to be a good army officer. My grandfather was principal of the most elite school in Kabul: Amani High School. He was well-known and I don't remember him smiling, ever! When he was at home, everyone was on their best behaviour, not only the kids but the grown-ups too, even my father. My father was always telling me how my grandfather's decision to put him into military school changed his life. To become an officer, you had to be either from a military family or have good connections. When my grandfather asked my father to choose a specific faculty in the military, he had no choice but to do so. My father, though he loved the military, loved his classmates even more. He wanted to be with his best mates and he chose a different faculty of the military academy, and my grandfather was not happy about it. My father told me how he argued with his father that he would not have his friends with him and how difficult it would be. However, the one thing Dad remembered and later told us was, 'When you are a good person and you have good manners, you will always attract friends and, more importantly, the right friends.'

Dad took this advice and he became an officer. He told us how it was the best decision, as most of his friends regretted the faculty they chose. It made life difficult for them, while Dad was living a better life and made so many friends; he still has those friends.

I asked my father one day, 'Dad, you listened to your father, he showed you the right path, you had better friends; you give us a good life, now I am asking you, what advice would you give me? What should I study, and who should I become to live a life and serve my people as you did?' I remember we were sitting in a bus, going home in a hot Pakistani summer, I was sitting on the seat next to a window, driving past a cricket ground. Dad replied, 'In my time, it was the military that was the option to serve my country, but for you, my advice would be to learn the English language, computers and science subjects.'

I took my father's advice, and for a short while I forgot about becoming a soldier. Though Afghanistan was ruled by the

Taliban, I always dreamed and strongly believed that one day the Northern Alliance would take over and once more we would have an independent nation – a nation which would allow education in all subjects, not just one religion.

Not only did my father give this advice, but he decided to send me to the best English and computer learning centre in the country. The fee was high, and they received funding from the American Fulbright organization, the UN, and more. Therefore this learning centre hired the best teachers. Though it was an Afghan institution, many Pakistani nationals also wanted to go and learn here. Their main focus was English language, but next to the English centre there was another building teaching IT or computer skills.

One of the reasons this centre was popular among Afghans and Pakistanis was the Fulbright Scholarship. This was an opportunity to go abroad and study or work. For many it was an escape from a hell such as Pakistan. For Afghans, it meant a new life abroad, somewhere to find freedom and be treated as a human, not a sub-human as in Pakistan. I never cared for all that. As a child, and a teenager, the only country I wanted to be in was Afghanistan. I wanted to fight the Taliban by joining Ahmad Shah Massoud's Northern Alliance.

In this centre for learning I learned so much, in particular from a man called Waheed Omar, my English teacher who taught us far more than just the language. Waheed Omar was a patriot, someone who I looked up to. His whole family was abroad, yet he was here. We had similar ideologies, and he hoped one day to go back and serve his nation. If my ambition was to serve my nation in the military, for him it was politics. He would take a higher level of English students. He liked me as a student who could speak fluent English. I remember one day he told me that if there was an award for the most fluent English speaker in that centre, he would give it to me. Compliments from an individual like him encouraged me to work harder. As a teenager, I was inspired by his patriotism, manners, and his easygoing approach to all students.

Waheed Omar loved cricket. He was fluent in many languages including Pashtu, Dari, English and Hindi/Urdu. He once punished me and my classmate for using the word 'prostitute'. Even though in no way was this word offensive, I think in the Afghan culture you are not allowed to use certain taboo words. He was the only teacher who was dressed well: shirt and trousers or jeans. He was always clean-shaved, which was rare among Afghan teachers. He would push us to speak English, in the class or outside; even for a chat he would always respond in English and expect us to speak in English, because he wanted us to learn the language by practising it daily. I guess he too wanted to practise, as well as wanting us to learn. He would always carry a dictionary. He kept the class interesting all the time. We used to look forward to his lessons. We were never bored with him. He would ask the same question multiple times until we learned it, but always had a smile on his face. His goal, unlike the other teachers, was to really teach and make sure we learned. He wouldn't mind teaching us a few minutes extra, and we didn't mind staying a few minutes extra to learn from him and improve our English and, most importantly, to listen to his stories which aimed to improve our critical thinking skills. Waheed Omar was so polite and well behaved that we even joked about him: jokes such as him not being able to talk to a girl, or that maybe he was not into girls. We used to make jokes about him, but mostly it was a compliment to him, even behind his back.

We admired him as patriotic Afghan. After the US invasion of Afghanistan, Waheed Omar went back and served in a different position in the Afghan government. Starting from translating for the head of the UN, Lakhdar Brahimi, later he became spokesman of the Afghan President, Hamid Karzai. Under President Ashraf Ghani he served as an ambassador to Italy, and recently he was appointed as a special advisor to the President. He never gave up, and always kept serving his nation. Waheed Omar still is one of those Afghan politicians who is not ethnocentric and selfish, but a patriot who only wants to see a peaceful, educated Afghan people. Today when I see him on TV or on twitter, just like Paul Rudd, the Hollywood actor, he hasn't aged a day! I hope to see him lead the country one day; he will only do good for the nation.

Back at the English learning centre, we weren't just working on speaking English, but we had classes on grammar, reading and writing, and every week there was a quiz to make sure we remembered what we had learned, and every three months a test. The centre aimed to teach you to write, read and speak fluent English in the space of eighteen months. The books were standard books provided by the IRC (International Rescue Committee), and the first English song I heard was 'The yellow of the taxis'! We used to know this by heart; it was part of our reading, listening quiz.

The English Waheed Omar taught me was formal, with a correct English accent. I have no idea what he thought of the culture whose words he imbued with such importance and gravity; perhaps it was the idealized world of some black-and-white movie, or the classics of English literature. The fact was that formal language and politeness sat comfortably with Afghan proprieties. A window had been opened onto another world, but one that I did not think would have much to do with my life. The English language offered a new perspective, nothing more. Learning the language was at the time an end in itself for me.

I made so many friends in this centre, some friends for life. But I didn't know how the unfortunate events of war and terrorism would affect me and these relationships. As there were no job opportunities for refugees in Pakistan, Afghans were looking for a better life abroad, Europe, America, Australia or anywhere, for their kids and themselves. Soon my good friends would migrate to Europe or America. One of my best friends would travel to the UK, and we lost contact for over a decade. Others went to Germany, Canada, UAE, Australia and Sweden. Ninety per cent of my friends from school and the centre left to live all over the world. All I have of them now is memories of playing cricket together or dodge ball.

We all learned cricket, as did many Afghans. Kids were playing it everywhere: at school, streets, backyards, everywhere. Also all Pakistani kids played it. I was quite good at it – I played at Kabul level – but when I had my job I couldn't play. When in Peshawar, I played for my school. Not official. I was an all-rounder, a fast bowler and opening batsman. The 1992 World Cup was big news everywhere. That was when I got interested. The Afghan under-19s got into the semi-finals of the World Cup, so really good.

I left Pakistan with an abiding love of cricket, but religion, on the other hand, began to impinge on my life in an increasingly unwelcome way. My family, though vaguely observant Moslems, were against religion spilling over very far into public life. It was part of who we were, but my father did not believe Islam to be exclusive of all other religions. His view was simple: To be good you did good, and a religion, or an interpretation of a religion, that told you to do bad things was a bad religion. This philosophy sustained me, but it was not one I could discuss in Peshawar. Although many of my fellow exiles were radicalized into the extremist view of Islam promoted by the Saudis and the Taliban, my spiritual journey was entirely in the opposite direction: towards the exit door.

In 1996 the Taliban swept to power, taking control of nearly all of Afghanistan, except the north. I rejoiced. Peace had come at last, and perhaps we could go home. My father said this was not so: he, and by extension the rest of us, would be far from safe under such a regime. However, as a 12-year-old I was going to be allowed to go to Kabul for a holiday with my cousins. At that age I was always required to have an escort if I wanted to go anywhere. I was jubilant at the chance to get away from Peshawar!

Chapter 3

Who are the Taliban?

The word 'Taliban' literally means students. 'Talib' student, 'Taliban' students. However, the 'Taliban' who are fighting aren't students, although they would like to think that they are students of religion (Islam). They believe they are fighting to defend Islam and Afghanistan; they believe in hardcore Sharia law and their goal is to implement Sharia law in Afghanistan, and possibility in the whole region.

The Taliban are a group of insurgents/terrorists who operate in Afghanistan and Pakistan. Their main objectives are to bring a barbaric rule to those countries, install Sharia law, and implement their rules and policies of killing and violence.

The Afghan Taliban are mainly formed from one Afghan ethnicity. Although a small number of their members come from other tribes of Afghanistan, their great majority come from the Pashtun ethnic group. The Afghan Taliban are over 95 per cent Pashtuns of Afghanistan, who are mainly from the southern provinces of the country. Their birthplace is Kandahar. Most of their leaders are from the south, including their founder and first leader, Mullah Omar (the blind terrorist who was killed by US forces).

The Taliban and other Mujahidin groups were created in the 1980s and supported/armed by the US government to fight the Soviet Union and defeat the Red Army. The United States at the time armed many parties who were representative of different tribes in Afghanistan. Almost all had one goal in mind – to defeat the Soviet Union in Afghanistan. The most effective ally of the USA was the group led by the Afghan national hero Commander Ahmad Shah Massoud. All the support provided by the US to the Mujahidin (or Holy Warriors), including arms and money, went through the Pakistani military. According to many books written about this time, most of these weapons were handed over to groups who were favourites of the Pakistan government or the Pakistani military intelligence services, the ISI. One of those favourites was Hekmatyar, another was the Taliban. They were and still are supported by the Pakistani government; they fight to bring back barbarism, which they believe to be in the national interest of Pakistan.

After the defeat of the Soviet Union, the Taliban were not as big as they are today and were not considered as much of a threat. The support they gained among the Afghan people, in particular with the Pashtuns, was due to ethnic civil wars in the country. Although many other parties struggled to keep up their war due to lack of funding or limited funding from their external donors, the Taliban received funds, arms and, more importantly, space from the ISI, in return for keeping Pakistani national interests in mind for as long as the Taliban remained in power in Afghanistan.

The Taliban leaders are mostly uneducated. The few who can read and write are those trained in Madrasas in either Pakistan or the tribal areas of Afghanistan. They don't believe in science or research, rather they believe in barbaric law and patriarchy. They believe women have no real rights. They believe that women must not be educated and that their sole purpose is to serve men and children at home. Women have to be escorted by a male wherever they go. So women are basically slaves.

They might marry as young as 10. In one of the intelligence-led operations we conducted against a Taliban leader, I witnessed something which still bothers me. In a night operation conducted by the SAS and Afghan special forces, we were sent to kill or capture a Taliban leader. After conducting the initial stages of the operations, I was interrogating everyone in the compound/ house. During this interrogation I was talking to a weak, white-bearded old man who could barely walk, the head of that family. I asked many questions related to the operation. I wanted to get answers for all the questions our task forces had for me. Of course he answered very vaguely, as they always do. It was my job to talk to other members of the family, male or female to get the correct answer. As I finished my interrogation, I was talking to this guy and told him that the story he was telling me did not match with what his granddaughter was telling. He replied to me saying, 'I do not have a granddaughter.' I then apologised to him and said, 'Oh maybe your daughter then?' I assumed that maybe he married his third wife a bit late – it's not uncommon for an old man – he looked to be about 70 – to have children in Afghanistan.

'My daughters are married and they live with their husbands,' he replied and looked offended.

I asked him then who was the child who was about 10 or 11 years old. He got really offended and angry. 'Why would you say that? That is my wife.' I told my sergeant major and told him that maybe I was wrong. He said, 'Well then ask him again, it couldn't be true. That cannot even be his daughter.' So I looked at him and asked again: 'I think you are mistaken, I am talking about the girl who is about 10 or 11 years old, and wearing a red dress with black scarf.'

Mostly in Afghanistan people don't know their age, especially in southern Afghanistan. If you ask an Afghan from a rural area their age, they might say, 'I am between 20 and 40.'

I asked the man again and he replied even more angrily. I decided I had to show him the girl, to be sure this was the girl we were talking about, so I took him to the room where the women were. When we interrogated individuals at Taliban or suspected Taliban houses, we separated the women from the men; usually men or one adult man in one room and the children and women in another. This was done for tactical questioning as well as to respect Afghan culture. When we got into the other room, I took his blindfold off and asked him to show me who he was talking about, to show me who was his wife. He pointed to the 11-year-old child. 'That's my wife,' he said.

I was sad for this kid who was being raped by this old man, but also sad for what would become of her when this old man died. Most of the women of the Taliban who are widowed at a young age, their lives are ruined. A girl born in a Taliban family is seen as a slave. As a sex slave they are abused on a daily basis, not only by their husbands, but their brothers, father and so on. When this girl's husband died, she would either be married to one of his brothers-in-law, or probably another old man with already three wives. This girl, and thousands of others born into Taliban families, suffer from the day they open their eyes to the day they die.

The Taliban have always condemned homosexuality. In their rule book, a homosexual must be either stoned or killed. They do not recognize any rights for homosexuals. However, almost all of them sleep with young boys when they are married to a woman, and they like to keep young boys, aged from 5 to 14, as sex slaves.

Most of the time they get these boys from their parents, with the promise to help them with religious studies, but in reality all they do is use them as sex slaves. I am saying this based on what I have witnessed.

During one of the special operations we conducted, we were supposed to either kill or capture a Taliban commander who had travelled from Pakistan to Afghanistan to give orders, and some other activities which posed a threat to NATO forces. He was on a mission to decide the fate of many Afghans who were held as Taliban prisoners. We had intel that he was staying in one of the compounds in the outskirts of a village in the Helmand province.

Most of the commanders sent from Pakistan to Afghanistan would keep a very low profile. In many cases they would not even have a bodyguard. It was the same with this Taliban leader. He was dressed in white 'dishdash', or the Afghan male dress, black vest coat, and black turban. He had a long beard and, like the rest of the Taliban commanders, he was fat.

As we were making our way to the target, we received intel that he was sleeping with three others just outside the compound. This was typical: in warm weather, people would normally sleep outside. The houses usually had no air-conditioning or fans; in most cases they didn't even have electricity. We landed a distance from the target, and after a long walk to the compound the assault team detained him quickly, to make sure we got him alive. I noticed that the other three individuals who were sleeping with the chubby Taliban commander were three minors aged between 6 and 10. After interrogating the commander, I went to speak to these three children who were sleeping with him. After interrogating them for a few minutes, they told me that they were being abused by him. Afghanistan is a place for Taliban commanders to come, kill innocent men, women and children, and keep sex slaves, often Afghan children. Most of these commanders had a wife in Pakistan and one in Afghanistan. It was sort of a holiday destination for them. For many, it was also their death destination. That's just one story of the Taliban; this was so typical of them.

Many people in the west think the Taliban are just a bunch of savages. In reality they are well-structured, well-funded, and have auxiliary support from other nations such as Pakistan, Iran, Saudi Arabia, United Arab Emirates and many other sympathisers from around the world. The greatest supporter or ally for the Taliban is Pakistan. Most of the Taliban's foreign fighters are Pakistanis, but there are fighters from all over the world, including from Iran, Russia and the Middle East. The Pakistani army were not only involved in the training and funding of Taliban fighters, but they were also responsible for planning attacks, appointing leadership, and their senior officers advised local Taliban leaders in Afghanistan. In one of the recent Taliban attacks, in which they targeted the Kunduz province of Afghanistan, there were hundreds of Pakistani Taliban fighters, including a Pakistani general. They were, of course, defeated, and hundreds of Taliban fighters were killed, many of them Pakistanis.

Afghanistan's other neighbour, Iran, has stepped up their support for the Taliban as well. Even though in the past Iran has supported anti-Taliban resistance, the Northern Alliance which was led by Commander Ahmad Shah Masoud, they are now supporting terrorist Taliban. The Iranians are however more active in providing logistical support to the Taliban. I have witnessed Irani military sleeping bags, weapons, rockets and improvised explosive devices. Their support for the Taliban isn't because they are a religious group, or because they want to promote terrorism against the Afghan government, but because they want to cause as much chaos as possible for the American forces in Afghanistan to make them withdraw from the country.

As we have seen from the recent killing of General Soleimani, the commander of Al-Quds of the Islamic Revolutionary guard, his main goal was to support any militia, in particular the Shiite groups, to continue their attacks on US forces so that they would eventually fail and withdraw from the region. General Soleimani was not just involved in Iraq and Syria, he was also actively attacking Afghan forces in Afghanistan.

When we talk about the Taliban, we must know that not all Taliban are fighting for the same cause their leaders claim they do. I have witnessed three types of Taliban during my work experience:

A - Religious extremist – These Taliban are those who fight for the cause they believe in. The hardcore ones. Most of the leadership, from high ranking in Quetta to local team leaders, are fighting for a cause they believe in. Most of the operations we conducted involving the capture or killing of leaders of the Taliban ended with the same result: the Taliban leader's death. Most of them will not give up, especially knowing that we will have evidence to put him behind bars for a long time.

B – External agents – This type of Taliban was formed of different nationalities, but were usually ISI agents, Pakistanis sent by the Pakistani intelligence services to advise and fight with the Taliban, aiming to kill Afghan, British and US soldiers. There were many suicide attackers arrested who were Pakistani nationals. One failed suicide attacker I was interrogating, who was arrested by the Afghan special forces before detonating himself, I asked him, 'Do you regret your actions? Now that you see everyone is Muslim, that they believe in the same god you do, that they pray and live as you do, do you still believe you were right?' He replied without hesitation: 'Even if you let me go now, I would wear my suicide vest and kill as many of your puppets as possible.' That was the mentality of most of these foreign Taliban. They strongly believed that the key to heaven was only available in Afghanistan. They were far from being a Muslim: they had no idea what Islam was, or for that matter what Christians or Jews believed in. They would spend all their lives in a closed community, a village, surrounded by people who would feed them only false information, to make them easy to use in the future; it is a culture where they have their own interpretation of Islam, a society where people's source of knowledge is narratives of events which occurred thousands of years ago, mostly made up. So when you present them with any other information, yours is the false one; it would not make sense to them, or even if it did, their minds would not allow them to think they had been wrong their whole life. The more you tell them, the more strongly they believe in their cause. Like the extremists, the only way to stop them is to kill them.

C – Those who have been recruited due to threats or poverty. This category of Taliban was mostly low-ranking. They were either forced or threatened to work for the Taliban, or they were doing so to get paid. Helmand province is one of the poorest places in the world. Most of the Taliban houses we raided where we located low-ranking Taliban members, after searching their houses you could not find food to last for the next two days. In one operation we conducted in the south of Afghanistan, we raided a house of low-level Taliban. There were no weapons, but we found enough evidence to confirm that they were supporting the Taliban. When talking to the women I noticed there was a new-born baby. Normally you feed a new-born with milk, but this family had no money for milk, the teat was full of tea – green tea. That's just water. I was curious to see if it was just the baby who was fed water instead of milk. When I went to their kitchen/ entrance of the house, I found boiled rice and a few pieces of bread. They had nothing in store, they literally had no more food for their lunch for the next day. They had no desire to fight, but they had to kill their own countrymen so their families could survive.

Chapter 4

The Islamic Emirate – *Emaraat-e-Islami*

I was so excited at going home, and being trusted to make such a journey, that I boarded the bus in a haze of glee and self-importance. Here I was, a man of the world, climbing aboard like an experienced international traveller. 'Excited' is an underestimate! Every refugee has gilded memories of home, and they are all the more unrealistic because of what has usually happened since he left. However, Afghanistan was finally at peace and I felt entitled to my optimism.

My disenchantment started almost immediately as I crossed the border. There by the road was a gaggle of ragged imps holding out begging bowls, aged between 4 and 10. Who was looking after them? Who allowed them to get into this state? On the road to Kabul I saw many such children. What was this country?

At the border crossing at Torkham there was always fear in the minds of Afghan refugees. Fear of being robbed by the corrupt Pakistani police and militia, fear of being beaten if you had no money, fear of being imprisoned for crimes that you had no idea about. It was a challenge of a one-kilometre walk which was the most important part of the trip.

I at least could speak the language; my cousin who was in his 20s could barely speak basic Urdu. He was more worried about crossing the border than I was, but he felt a bit lucky to have me to act as his translator. Although it's a one kilometre walk, it was the last few minutes that were the issue. That's where a crowd of corrupt Pakistani police and militia were waiting, keeping an eye out for Afghans who looked nervous or well-dressed so they could get some money out of them. As Afghans, we were trying to not make eye contact with them and just hoping they would not stop us. Usually we would have a secret pocket to make sure they didn't find our money and steal it.

We crossed the border without any problems, not sure what it was about us that made them let us go and not rob us.

As we approached the Afghan side of the border there were no soldiers, only Taliban wearing dishdashes, each one's beard longer than the other, non-existent discipline, militants standing wherever they wanted, weapons on their shoulders. What surprised me at that time was to see Pakistani soldiers roaming around the Afghan side of the border without any problems, yet Taliban were not allowed to cross to their side. I heard that the Taliban were Pakistani puppets, but this was low even for the Taliban.

Seeing that there was no official border between the two countries, or that Pakistan had such control over the Taliban, was depressing, I felt sad: it wasn't the image I imagined or wanted to see. Even though I disliked the Taliban, I still felt my nation was humiliated.

I watched as Afghan refugees came from the other side of the border. They were heavily searched, and abused physically, verbally, and emotionally. They were robbed of their money and beaten. Man, woman or child, old or young, no one was spared as they were subjected to the humiliation of the Pakistani army. It was a sad scene which I will never forget. But the Pakistanis entering the country were never even questioned! They could walk into Afghanistan without any hassle. No passport check, no visa check, you just walked into this landlocked country with no owner.

My cousin and I kept walking. As you crossed the border there was a further 15 to 20 minutes' walk to get to the bus stop for the trip to Kabul. It was a long journey which I was not looking forward to. As we arrived at the bus stop, crossing a market of vehicle spare parts, there were about fifteen drivers asking us to get into their car. But these cars were too expensive for us. Me and my cousin chose to travel in the bus, an old 1980s Mercedes bus, which was packed! It was shabby compared to the Pakistani buses.

For a few miles the road was paved. It was a nice drive. But as soon as we got closer to the city of Jalalabad it became a dirt track! The bus couldn't travel more than fifteen miles an hour. And it was dusty – it was a nightmare! There were no services, or if there were one or two, the food would poison you. That's why my mom had packed some boiled eggs and bread for me. That was my food for the whole day, breakfast, lunch and dinner. It was a long, slow, bumpy journey.

All the valleys looked similar, but my eyes were looking for just one. I remembered that particular valley because when I was a kid my father and I were travelling to a different province of Afghanistan and on our way we were stopped by militias. Their leader travelled with us and all the way to his next destination he was sitting next to me and he talked to me. As a child, knowing that this man was a killer, a murderer, was terrifying. The memory of that area stayed with me and that's how I knew Kabul was close.

The trip to Kabul, which takes around two hours nowadays when the roads are paved, took us nine hours back then. As we approached the paved streets of Kabul, you could not see many cars around, and because of that the air was so clean! Unlike

Peshawar, which was so polluted that you struggled to breathe. It was a lovely fresh smell. But the city was quiet. Almost too quiet! Coming from such a noisy city as Peshawar, this was a shock.

In Peshawar people had the choice of shaving, wearing what they wanted, and women could walk alone without a family escort. But in Kabul there was a sense of fear around; you could feel it! There was no life in the city, it was mostly a ghost city. You could see people, but there were few smiles. Every man, woman and child looked down, the city was robbed of its happiness, life was a struggle. All the men had long beards, you could not see anyone wearing jeans, only dishdashes. And women? Not many were to be seen. They were not allowed to go out. If you did spot a woman, she was completely covered with burka, and had a male escort who would have been a member of her family. Crazy Sharia law!

In Kabul I hung out with my cousin. He was the same age as me. You could sense the oppressed life the people were living, depressed at the endless religious dictates. Women under the Taliban, it seemed, had become ghosts. It was as though every citizen was under a cloud.

We stayed at our grandfather's house. We had a beautiful garden, although now it was not as pretty as in my grandfather's time. Now there was barely enough water for the people; trees would not be the priority here. Despite that, it brought back so many childhood memories. When I was a child, the house would always have guests. My cousins, their kids, we would all play together, but war has taken all that away.

The little garden, the vineyard which my grandfather took care of, was gone! The flowers which he grew with love were almost nonexistent. The atmosphere was not as I remembered. In one house, three families lived: my uncle, cousins and their families, and one cousin whose father was killed earlier in the civil war. It was packed. During the war, families wanted to stay close to each other, not only to save on rent, but also to make sure they could reach out to each other easily, support each other financially, and provide food if needed. Financially my cousins were struggling. They did not have food at home for two days. It was mostly work the day, then find food for the day after. If they failed, the family had to stay hungry, even with food rationing.

But the location was beautiful! It was high up in the great mountains of Kabul. You could see the whole city from the wide windows of the living room. And the view was beautiful at night. Even though there were no lights in the city, it was still something to stare at, in those scary quiet nights of Taliban-era Kabul.

One day we went to a football match. As we waited for kick-off, the mood was upbeat, as if in the stadium people would be able to shake off their day-to-day worries and depression. My cousin and I jostled our way to a good vantage point on the terraces, receiving some good-natured cuffs along the way. Suddenly the crowd went quiet. We strained to see what was happening. A man was marched under armed guard into the centre of the field. He was ordered to kneel. There was a silence I never thought possible in a crowd this size. The man's crimes were read out over the tannoy. The words rang out over the dumb crowd. I looked at my cousin in confusion. He just shook his head. After the words came the shot.

I did not know how to react. Only a moment before I had been excited at the football game. Now I was in shock. It was the first time in my life to visit a stadium, and now it was my first time seeing someone get shot in a stadium. I was cheering for my cousin's favourite team, and this horrific thing happened to ruin my experience. My body was shaking in horror, but my cousins on the other hand forgot about it almost immediately and carried on as if nothing happened. Not just my cousins, but most of the people in the stadium. The corpse was carried off. The crowd slowly came back to life in whispers, then mutters, then talk.

The two teams came out and the players' names were announced on the same tannoy. How was I supposed to watch a football match after that? Though I never recovered my effervescence of before, we began to comment on the game, and then cheer our team on, as though we might as well make the best of this rotten world.

That Friday, my cousin and I were bicycling about when we were accosted by a group of Mullah Omar's thugs, the 'Amre Bel Maruf wa Nehmenkar', which supposedly carried out the orders of their thug leaders, Mullah 'Blind' Omar. They screamed at us, 'Why aren't you at prayers?', grabbed us and frogmarched us into a mosque where we were whipped along with a lot of other children they had caught.

After we were beaten, we managed to sneak away and jumped on our bikes, pedalling back home as quickly as we could. As we turned a corner not far from my cousin's home we came across some more Taliban thugs standing in the road, who tried to catch us. I don't know how we got round them, but my pedalling was powered by terror. I thought I was going to be killed, like the man in the football stadium. Maybe I was being a bit dramatic, but the fear was there, the shock was still there: God knows what would have happened if we had been caught. Luckily we lost them and did not stop till we got home. For us and the rest of the city, we were dealing with such terror on daily basis.

After spending a few weeks in Kabul it was time to go back to being a refugee, back to being a foreigner, but safe and with my parents and siblings. It was a mixed feeling to go back. I felt happy to see my family and to be away from the terror of terrorist Taliban, but I was sad to be leaving my country again. I was going to be a refugee again in a land which played a significant role in destroying my country and its infrastructure.

On the bus back to Peshawar I burned with anger. My vision of Afghanistan had been soiled by the Taliban. I asked myself how I could free it from these demons. My dream of becoming a soldier, a servant of Afghanistan, was becoming a strong desire. I decided that whenever I got a chance, I would join the Afghan forces. At the time it seemed impossible for Afghanistan to be free from the Taliban and have its own national security force. The only thing was hope, a hope which was also known as Ahmad Shah Massoud! The leader of the Northern Alliance. I hoped that he would continue fighting for us, for the future of Afghanistan.

Back in Peshawar, I soon fell back into the usual routine, and one day a few years later the hope that had been Commander Massoud's Northern Alliance died. In 2001, two days before 9/11, I was 16 years old and on the bus home from school when I heard some men saying that Al Qaeda had assassinated Ahmad Shah Massoud.

Massoud had started the resistance for a free, democratic Afghanistan from his early university days. He had devoted his life to fight for his people, so that all ethnicities would have the same rights, and both men and women. He wanted Afghans to prosper and build a modern Afghanistan. He was more than a hope for us, he was a symbol of resistance.

Despite my customary discretion, I could not help but weep at the news. He was a Tajik like me, and – in so far as any warlord could be – a hero to my family. Although he was Tajik, he never believed in serving one ethnicity, he believed in a fair Afghanistan. For many Pakistanis, however, he was the devil himself; he was the man standing against Pakistani hopes to have Afghanistan as their fifth state. As I started weeping over the death of this incredible man, a Pakistan army officer approached me and asked, 'Is there anything wrong, my son?' I replied, 'Yes, our hero Massoud died.' He did not expect me to give this reply and started shouting at me for crying and feeling sad for the death of the man who was standing in the way of making Afghanistan one of their territories, a man who had probably killed many people in the defence of his people and country. He started to beat me when I told him through my tears that Massoud had been murdered, that he was a great man and a great leader. The more he beat me the more I extolled Massoud's virtues. Thankfully the other people on the bus intervened and got the army officer to lay off. I was a young boy, desperate to have my own self-reliant country. I was worried that I would be a refugee forever. I was worried about my people back home. I could not bear the thought of Afghanistan under the barbaric Taliban regime. However, I resolved never to let my feelings master me like that again.

Two days later my life would change forever when thousands of miles away two huge skyscrapers were destroyed. Thousands of innocent Americans were murdered by the very same terrorist organization that assassinated the leader of the Northern Alliance: Osama Bin Laden's Al-Qaeda.

My father used to tell me that his dreams would come true if he saw a free Afghanistan again in his lifetime. 'We are saved!' he told me.

I asked, 'How are we saved? Massoud is dead, Dad.'

He replied, 'Now you will see! Mark my words: that President Bush will destroy the Taliban for allowing such an act! Soon we will be able to go home again!'

I was doubtful. But he was right: soon I would be free, and NOT a refugee, after a very long nine years.

Chapter 5

The Interpreters

When you hear the word 'interpreter' you may think of a person who translates one language to another; someone who interprets languages. However, to a terrorist it has a totally different meaning. They would call them the infidels' puppets, the infidels' eyes and ears, spies, traitors and so on.

If you ask an Afghan civilian what an interpreter is, they will give a different answer again. An interpreter is a pimp! This is the worst curse word there is in Afghan society. It doesn't get any lower than a pimp in Afghanistan. And they would also call an interpreter a puppet, an infidel, and a 'murtad' – meaning a very bad Muslim or a Muslim who has converted to Christianity or any other religion.

If you ask an Afghan military officer or NCO what an interpreter is, they will probably give different answers. Some will call them teachers or instructors, others will call them infidels, dogs, Christians, or other offensive words. Each will have a story.

Among Americans or other NATO forces you will probably find more positive descriptions of interpreters. Americans looked after their interpreters, in particular the special forces. It was almost every interpreter's dream to be assigned to work with the special forces. One reason for that was they would receive military training, carry a rifle, and be allowed to kill Taliban. They also received better kit and got paid well. Interpreters who worked for the regular army were always jealous of the interpreters who worked for the special forces.

To work for the special forces you needed fluency in the English language, security clearance, and obviously it helped if you hated the terrorist Taliban.

There were other things to consider too. My brother worked for ODA or US army special forces, also known as the green berets. He had the privilege of shooting terrorist Taliban, but it made him famous, which put his life in danger.

I know many interpreters of the special forces who have been killed, or in some cases their families targeted. Working with the SF wasn't entirely a privilege, it was also more likely you would get killed. Not that regular army interpreters were living a risk-free life: the casuality rate of interpreters was actually higher in the regular army than it was with the SF. Up to 2012, over 2,000 US army local interpreters have been killed in action. I myself have lost sixteen very good friends who were interpreters in this bloody war on terrorism. Two were beheaded by the overweight Mullah Dadullah who like the rest of the Taliban leaders used to issue 'tickets to heaven' to his fighters promising them entrance to heaven after a suicide attack. (A ticket to heaven! That's how ignorant the Taliban fighters are: they believe that a human being has control over heaven.) How did I find out about their execution? Through Bluetooth videos. Terrorist Taliban killed them and then sold videos of their beheading in the markets of Kabul. Then it was transferred onto mobile phones, after which it was sent to my phone. Needless to say, I was shocked. No matter how used to death you get, when you see your best buddies beheaded, it is more painful than you can imagine.

Later I heard that there were videos out there of interpreters being interviewed by the Taliban. I did not know that it was the same two interpreters, my friends Yahya and Achekzai. They were begging for their lives, asking the mullah to forgive them, to allow them to go back to their families and they would never work for the Americans again. Yahya was saying to this terrorist leader, 'Please Mullah Saheb, I promise you that if you let me go now, I will never join their ranks again. I am a Muslim, have mercy on me as a Muslim.' His skin was pale, you could see the fear in his eyes, he knew he was in the hands of a bunch of barbaric terrorists, yet he still tried to find a way to escape.

Unfortunately, this was a Taliban propaganda video. They knew the value of interpreters. Instead of forgiving them, he announced that the two interpreters were spies and according to Sharia law they must be beheaded. And that's what happened.

One thing I was sure of was that I would keep fighting and make sure that Yahya and Achekzai, or many other interpreters whose names were never mentioned, didn't die for nothing. Terrorist Taliban always assumed that by killing interpreters they would inflict fear in our hearts and that we would stop working. Little did they realise that the more brothers we lost the more motivated we became to carry on our fight, to make a difference and make sure these terrorists wouldn't control our country.

A few months later we were sitting in our 'interpreters' accommodation' at Camp Phoenix, which was literally a tent! There were roughly thirty interpreters there. One had just returned from a mission and he looked so happy and you could see that he just wanted to share his news: 'Mullah Dadullah is killed! That bastard is burning in hell now,' he shouted with a big smile on his face. I too was happy, relieved and emotional as I heard the news. Because we were so loud and shouting, an American officer walked in, worried that something might have happened. 'What's going on guys? Is everyone okay?' he asked, and everyone shared the brilliant news. It meant a lot to us interpreters, as Dadullah was targeting interpreters on a daily basis. Unfortunately he was just one monster out of a bunch of thousands. Still, to see him get killed, dishonourably, cheered us at least temporary. His evil name always reminds me of my two friends and brings tears to my eyes... May they rest in peace.

Thousands of interpreters got killed, but it was never really broadcast by the world media or even local media. Interpreters were hated by almost everyone in Afghanistan, some because of their beliefs, some because of jealousy due to the pay they were receiving. The great majority of these interpreters were between the ages of 18 and 25. They were mostly single, some were engaged, a few were married and left behind orphans and widows.

Most Afghans believed that interpreters were the cause of the civilian casualties. They believed that it was the interpreters who killed the Taliban and caused civilian casualties. It was said that interpreters kidnapped women from their homes and supplied them to the Americans.

The interpreters in fact played an important role in avoiding civilian casualties. One of their roles was to serve as liaison between the US and Afghan forces/militias and to act as a cultural advisor to the mentor teams. Afghan interpreters used to advise on the culture of the people for counter-insurgency purposes. Americans did not understand Afghan culture, especially at the start of the war. They did not take care not to offend the Afghan people, and then they would get offended and confused when the Afghans did things in a different way than the Americans would expect.

It was the Afghan interpreters who provided information on cultural issues to avoid misunderstandings between the village, tribal leaders, Afghan forces and US forces. In this way they ultimately reduced casualties.

The role of interpreters didn't finish on the battlefield. On return to their home towns, they had to fight other issues, support their families economically, fight the ignorance of people who always misunderstood the interpreters, and worry about being kidnapped. Of course back in their home towns they were easier targets for the Taliban since they had no NATO forces to protect them. Many interpreters' families were taken hostage, many were threatened, to provide intelligence against the US forces or be killed. Many interpreters lost members of their families. Any interpreter who was threatened was in a very tricky situation. Whatever happened they were going to lose something. The policy of the US and NATO forces was, if an interpreter was threatened, they were to be terminated from their job immediately. This happened to many interpreters working for the British forces. The interpreter would not only lose his job and struggle financially, he would also have to deal with the threat, either from terrorists or other thugs, without any support. Back in 2007 the reward was higher to kill interpreters than it was for US soldiers. The Taliban knew the importance of the interpreters.

There were of course good and bad interpreters. Some couldn't even speak English and were hired in desperation due to the need for language experts on missions. This, on many occasions, backfired. In some cases the US or NATO allies would have been better off not to use interpreters at all. I have witnessed many times where interpreters couldn't understand what the US soldiers were saying and instead of asking again they translated something completed differently. Then the Afghan counterpart would give an answer to what the interpreter was asking, not the mentor. No-one would get an answer to their question and both would think that their counterpart was incompetent. Such misunderstandings led to many problems and created mistrust between the Afghan and US forces.

Some Afghans pronounce 'P' as 'F'. They just cannot say it! On one occasion we had to travel from one province to another for mission purposes. We had a colonel with us. After waiting a few days at the airport, it was finally time to go. However, the colonel was taking his time to get ready. One of the officers asked an interpreter to go and see if the colonel was ready. The interpreter rushed to his room and a few minutes later he ran back out of breath and said: 'Sir, the colonel is fucking, and he won't take long.' All of us looked at each other and one sergeant said, 'Alright, the colonel is getting some!' Our first guess was that the colonel was getting laid, but then we realised he was a man of discipline and wouldn't do that. The officer who was standing with us asked him again: 'Who is fucking? How? What do you mean?' and the interpreter replied, 'He is fucking his bags to get ready.'

Interpreters had different categories with different security clearances. This was not based on merit. Much depended on whether one had an Afghan passport or American or British. The difference in pay was from $400 USD to $20,000 USD a month. Crazy! There were local nationals who got paid between $400 and $2,500 a month, local nationals who were in the frontline, risking their lives, advising US mentors, and we have lost thousands of them. Then there was category one, or CAT-1, who got paid around $10,000 a month for having a US green card. They were there just for meeting with elders, not for their spoken language abilities – they were arrogant! CAT-2 was those who had an American passport, with security clearance; they got paid about $12,000 a month. They knew nothing about Afghanistan, mostly they were there just to earn the money and kill time. You could more often find them at the chow hall or eating kebabs at the kebab shops in the bases. Then there was CAT-3, who had top secret clearance and got paid over $20,000 a month. All they had to do was attend one or two meetings in six months, and the rest of the time just chill. They didn't have to pay any tax and their language abilities were horrible! They were Afghans who had lived almost all their lives in the US and had no connection with contemporary Afghanistan. The Americans trusted them more than the Afghans who lived in Afghanistan itself. So many bombings occurred because of the misjudgement of these individuals.

A problem with CAT-1, 2, and 3 interpreters was that they could speak fluent English but not Dari or Pashtu. They were mainly hired out of the desperation of contractors to supply CAT interpreters. One of the reasons for the high wages was that they would be going into a hostile country; the reality was, all they did was stay in camps, eat kebabs and pizza and drink coffee. It was the local nationals who did the fighting and paid the ultimate price.

For local nationals it was very difficult to get a job. They either had to pay their first months' salary to the person who would help them get a job or wait years to get a call.

A very good friend of mine, who was the only child of his family, very poor, wanted to get a job to help his father with bills. He was subcontracted to provide translation services with the 82nd Airborne Division during the 2005 election in the south of Afghanistan. His name was Faheem, a 21-year-old boy, happy and full of life. Many times he woke me up early in the morning to play volleyball. Or in the evening. He had dreams of serving his parents, who took care of him and were living in poverty.

We were tasked to leave early in the morning on patrols to provide security for the people of Afghanistan to choose their next president, by supporting the national army in targeting Taliban commanders who were a threat to the election commission.

Faheem and I hadn't worked together long, but we were on the same wavelength and had become firm friends. One day we were in an army vehicle driving down the road to patrol an area mostly in control of the Taliban. It was during Ramadan, and it was summer in a very hot part of the country. On the morning of that day I remember his face looked so bright and I joked with him: 'Faheem, you look very handsome today.' He said that I was in love with him and that maybe I am into boys. That day the weather was very hot, and during the patrol, which was around noon time, fasting made him thirsty. Many times I suggested he should break his fast and drink some water, but he refused. As a devoted Muslim he wanted to fast that day.

By now I had seen a lot. I had been involved in many operations which had resulted in the killing of hundreds of terrorists all over the country – usually Taliban. But I was still unprepared for this.

I guess the heat got to him and he decided to open the window of his vehicle to get some air and maybe his head was half out of the window when the IED detonated. All of a sudden dust was everywhere. I was in another vehicle and as I heard the blast I never for a second thought it would be him. At first I thought it was our Humvee and that perhaps I was gone. After a few seconds, I looked around and I was fine, and so were my colleagues. We didn't get out of the Humvee as there were shots being fired. We all were preparing for another possible attack as the dust settled. Eventually I got out and noticed that one Humvee was in pieces. I wanted to check on the others and I noticed that two Humvees ahead of me was the vehicle Faheem was in. That's when my heart started beating fast and everything around me became invisible. I had to run, I didn't care about the bullets flying around me. As I ran towards him he was facing the other way and I could only see the back of his head. When I got there, I saw it was Faheem lying there, I could recognize him. He was covered in blood. His legs were fine but half of his head and face were gone… The picture of that moment is still in my head. I still see him lying there, with his bloody body armour and lifeless body. I don't remember what was happening around me, the only thing I see is him lying on the floor. I am still haunted by it today. You never think it is going to be you, but when death comes to someone close, you realise it could easily be you too.

I am not sure how I got back to base, but the news travelled fast. His father was devasted. He could not bear it. As strong as he pretended to be, a year later he died, leaving a widow. To this day the US armed forces have not paid the life insurance money which was supposed to be given by the US to Faheem's parents.

I always see and remember the faces of all those interpreters who were close to me and were killed in action. One of the reasons I decided to write this book was to tell the world, in particular the Afghan people, that the interpreters who they always hated played a big role in the democracy they have today. They sacrificed their lives, they reduced casualties, and made a difference in the war on terror so that future generations of Afghanistan don't have to see such threats.

Some interpreters were Taliban sympathisers. They were sort of spies to the Taliban. Some even hated the international forces, despite getting paid by them and making a living out of them. Most of these Taliban sympathisers that I met were either raised in refugee camps in Pakistan or were from villages ruled by Taliban extremism and ignorance, and raised by parents who were mostly illiterate yet were interpreting the Quran to their kids. There were many interpreters who were Pakistanis, since it was easy to attain Afghan identity paperwork. They called themselves Afghan and surprisingly passed the 'screening test' and the US army security checks.

On one occasion when working with US army special forces, the Green Berets, we got ambushed four times in a valley. The details of these operations were not shared with regular armed forces, they were known only to the special operations community. A few days later we were hanging out in our building which was for interpreters, and one of the US special forces walked in and started roughing up this interpreter. We were of course not happy and wanted an explanation, so one of the interpreters stepped in and asked the US service man to stop hitting him and tell us why he would beat an interpreter. The service man said, 'Don't worry, once we deal with him we will explain why we are doing this.' Later that day we were told that the past four ambushes happened because of him as he was sort of a spy to the Taliban. Since he was a new interpreter, we didn't know him well and it made us worried that such interpreters could also leak our identity.

And then there were interpreters like Raffi, who was working at camp Souter, a British camp in Kabul where all the interpreters were being hired and sent to southern Afghanistan. He was corrupt and used to ask interpreters to pay him their first month salary as a fee so he could make sure they would pass the initial language test. Many interpreters who could speak fluent English couldn't get a job because they didn't have the money to bribe. Many interpreters were not corrupt and believed it was morally wrong to pay this interpreter to get a job. Many of the interpreters who paid and got a job could barely speak English beyond greetings. It made the Afghan national army look stupid and created many misunderstandings. Because of such interpreters, the rest suffered and some paid the ultimate price by sacrificing themselves before even getting paid.

Chapter 6

Old Home, New Life –
Khana e Sabeq, zindagee naw

fghanistan was ablaze. Every night my family gathered around the TV and watched images of the victorious Northern Alliance, aided by their new, old, allies the Americans, bundle the Taliban out of power. We would cheer (though not too loudly) and I would pester my parents to return to Kabul.

'No, no. It's too early,' they said. 'Let the dust settle.'

I could hardly contain myself. We had waited so long for this, and I could not believe their cautious attitude. I shouted at them, 'Let *me* go then! I don't want to spend another minute in this Godforsaken country.'

'How will you get there? You don't have the fare!' they replied. Back and forth our argument raged. Only when I threatened to walk all the way to Kabul did they take me seriously and give me the money for a bus ticket. I was overjoyed. Joy to not only have a new free Afghanistan, but see my relatives, my cousins, and see my gorgeous Afghanistan again.

It was spring 2002 when I finally went home. I was 17 and giddy with optimism. The long hard winter had been banished and everywhere looked and smelt like new life. It felt free. Free of barbarism, free of oppression, free of terrorism. Little did I know that this would NOT be an overnight struggle.

When I reached Kabul, I stayed with my cousin again, and revelled at coming home. By the middle of the summer the rest of my family, with my encouragement and a bit of pressure, decided it was safe enough for them to join me.

Now we had to rebuild a life for ourselves. The retired colonel set up an auto shop and car parts business. I will never know how much Dad wished he was back in the army, but with his customary courage he threw himself into this new life. I wish it could have been enough for me, but it just wasn't. I did not come back to Kabul to patch up old cars. I had always wanted to follow his footsteps into the army and pestered him to let me join up, let me serve my people and my country the way he had served for over three decades.

My long-suffering father explained patiently that the Afghan army no longer existed. He took me to visit his old army comrades, now living in varying states of poverty around Kabul. Each shrugged regretfully and explained that there was no Afghan army, merely a façade of so-called 'divisions' which were in reality the militias of the victorious warlords of the Northern Alliance given a superficial makeover. He took me to one of his old friends at the Ministry of Defence – it looked nothing like a ministry of defence but rather a base for the Northern Alliance. I explained how much I wanted to serve my country and to pursue the dream of following my father. Maybe in a few years time, they averred, things would be more normal. 'Better wait my boy. You are young, you will get a chance to serve your country, it doesn't necessarily have to be through the military. There are other ways to serve.'

If my father thought that would dissuade me he was wrong. There *was* a proper army in Afghanistan: the US army. If could not serve in the Afghan Army, I would work with them. I believed

– and I still believe – that the US army served to make this nation a better place for all.

I heard that the Americans were looking for interpreters. My English had improved as I had picked up quite a lot of vocabulary in Pakistan. But how would I apply? Where would I start? I knew many contractors, many people, who could have helped me get a job as an interpreter, but all, one way or other, were a let-down. I had to rely on myself. I had to be the one to make a move and work hard if I wanted to be what I wanted to be. After asking around I finally learned that the Americans were hiring only in the neighbouring province of Kabul, Parwarn Province, Bagram Airbase. The base at Bagram was heavily guarded, and I had no idea how to get a pass.

After completing numerous CVs and making numerous attempts to get a job as an interpreter, I failed. But my will to work for the people who were helping my people was not going to be ended easily. I was strong and patient. There had be another way.

I discovered that a local construction company was carrying out works at the camp. I announced to my puzzled father that I was leaving the workshop to go and work for them, in what was a much lowlier job than my current one. Almost immediately I regretted it. I spent all day doing back-breaking work, building berms and digging ditches miles away from any US army personnel. Any time I tried to wander away I was shouted at by my foreman. The Americans kept away from the Afghan workers and there were no opportunities to mingle.

After a couple of months, I happened to be working near the gates and saw a group of soldiers coming in. They looked a bit different from the other American soldiers I had seen so far (mostly, it has to be said, at a distance). They were bigger, they moved in a different way, with less swagger and more economy. They had long beards, wore baseball caps, and carried some serious equipment. Long beards, baseball caps and Oakleys! It looked like they had just come off patrol. I was not going to let this chance slip. I told myself, 'This is my chance, it's now or never! This is the difference between digging ditches or getting the chance to put the terrorists in their holes.' So I flung my shovel down, jumped out of the trench I was digging, and approached what appeared to be their officer.

The man stopped and looked at me. 'Please sir, I want to work for you guys, I would like to be your interpreter,' I said in what I hoped was my best English. The man looked at me. A small commotion broke out from the direction of the ditch. The officer looked towards it. It was my foreman: 'What the hell do you think you're doing? Get back here at once!' I shouted back: 'I did not come here to work for you!'

I looked back at the officer, who stared back at me calmly. He looked me up and down, then said simply, 'Will you kill Taliban if you see one?' I answered enthusiastically in the affirmative.

'Alright then, come with me.'

I followed him.

Chapter 7

'The Eagle Shits Today' – *Aghaz e naw*

The officer took me into a large room and introduced me to the team. They were all welcoming and friendly. After a couple of hours of questions and a photo taken, I was astonished when the officer turned to me and handed me a hundred dollars: 'Here's some taxi money. Come back tomorrow and we'll get you started.' A hundred dollars! Taxi Money? At the time that would feed an Afghan family for a month. So not only was I going to get the job I'd dreamed of since I was a child, but I was going to get well paid for it. I was very happy. On my way back to Kabul I felt like a weight was lifted. I was going to be able to serve my people and my country.

I worked with this team for about six months over the winter of 2003/4, mostly going on operations in Kapisa province. My brother, once he heard what I was doing and what I was earning, also became an interpreter. I did not want him to work with the security forces, because I knew how dangerous it was. I was already facing a lot of risk, where before any operation I always wondered if I was going to come back alive. I did not want this for my brother, I wanted him to follow a different path: education! Anyway, for both of us, our English language skills improved rapidly. I improved mine by working and practising with Americans; my brother would get up at 4 am and walk for hours to get to an English language course to learn the language. His desire to serve his country was even greater than mine.

I also started to learn the finer arts of interpretation. It was not enough to be a translator of words. Western men also use different body language, and I had to translate this too when questioning Afghans for them.

The difference between interpreting and translating became crystal clear very early in my new career when we were interrogating a detainee picked up during an operation. The Afghan kept going on about something trivial – I can't remember what it was – and Dan, the American I was interpreting for, was getting irritated by his pleading.

He stared at the detainee, 'Tell him I don't give a fuck about his bullshit story.'

'What?' I said.

'Tell him.'

'I *can't*,' I said. 'That's a rude word. I mean *nobody* says that to people.'

'Fuck, Eddy, you telling me nobody fucking swears in this fucking country?'

'Well not like that. I mean that would be really insulting.'

'Ok just tell him the best way you can.'

So I did, politely, tell the Afghan that the soldier did not care. The Afghan looked nonplussed, and shrugged. I went on to explain in greater depth that the man asking him the questions *really* did not care about this particular matter.

As I talked, Dan stared at me in incredulity.

'Jesus Eddy! Are you telling him your life story? Forget it man!'

The detainee and I looked at each other as Dan wandered off. This was going to be harder than I thought.

My other job was to listen in on the Taliban radio chatter and warn the Americans what was going on behind the hills, or in the next village. Would they be attacked soon? How close were they? It was not long before I found myself being given extra responsibility by the soldiers I worked with. I loved it: it was a mark of trust. I was their eyes and ears in the war against the Taliban. Being an interpreter was not just about translations. We had more responsibilities and with each responsibility I learned something new and I kept growing as a person. The people I was working with were the best mentors I could have ever asked for. Not only that, but as a 17-year-old boy I could not have asked for any better friends to have around me. I was learning about the vast cultural differences between Afghan and western societies and I was learning about life in general. Every day was not just another mission, but a learning opportunity for me.

Sometimes the intensity of a situation could be wearing. On one patrol we were involved in a vicious firefight. Afterwards I felt completely drained. I don't know how the others felt, but the barked commands, the short fuses and the anger had been hard to translate, especially during heavy gunfire. I had to tone everything down. I was getting accustomed to the way these Americans were used to not taking offence, but it made my life as their interpreter hard, especially when the shit hit the fan.

After six months my team was rotated out of Afghanistan, but they handed me over to the new team, with the highest recommendation. My reputation grew quickly amongst the Americans. Perhaps it was because I was no ordinary 'terp': I shared their goals, and above all I hated the Taliban with an intensity that outdid even their own. This was, and is, no act.

I particularly hated the way the Taliban treated women. I was once at a checkpoint when a car drove up with several men and one woman in it. As the Afghan soldiers were searching the car I kept translating. I was speaking to the Afghan National Army soldier in Dari. As I was translating, I heard women crying in the back. I was worried and assumed that the Afghan army soldier must have done something to make her cry. I went on to ask her in Pashtu, which was the local language, 'What's happening sister?' As she heard that, she burst into tears. I then asked her in Pashtu why she was crying. She said it was the first time she had heard Dari in years. Under the Taliban regime she had been forced to marry one of the men in the car. While the car was being searched I took her a little distance away and said, 'You don't have to stay here you know, there is no shame in going home.' She said that she would like to go home, but her whole life was now here in the south, with the children she had with this man. What could she do? She got back into the car with her husband and his friends and drove off in silence. This was just one story, probably not even a sad one compared to all the tragedies and abuse that occurred in the Taliban era. Just like her, thousands of women were treated as an animals, as servants. They were forced to marry men who were older than their fathers, forced to remarry their brothers-in-law, kept like prisoners, raped by multiple men of the same family, abused physically.

Not long after that I was chosen to interpret at COIN, the American Counter Insurgency Academy in Kabul. I met some really smart people there, including Captain Brandon Anderson who had served in Iraq and thought deeply about the problem of counter-insurgency, and Captain Helmer. I clicked immediately with them and the others, becoming the interpreter of choice for high-ranking officers. Working for the counter-insurgency academy was one of the best 'learning' years of my life. I learned not only through books, but the officers I was working with each had something to share, and every experience they shared was a new lesson to me. I always had a desire to talk to each officer and pick their brains. Everything they said helped me understand the war and the politics of it differently. They also taught me many of the key skills which I would later need while studying at university in the United Kingdom. It was almost like an advanced sort of a lecture. I realized that all these years I was working as an interpreter for the forces helping my nation, I was also attending university, learning something new every day. In fact, when back in the UK, studying for my undergraduate and postgraduate degrees, none of my lecturers came close to the level of the knowledge of the officers I worked with. I learned more from them in a year than I did in five years at university.

At some point in my time with the Americans, I realized that I had changed. I don't know when their point of view started to become mine. Perhaps it was when I was queuing at the base. To stand in line for something is a deeply un-Afghan way to behave, but there was no way I would have jumped the queue. It would have been rude, uncivilised even. My cousins teased me when I stood in line at a shop outside the base, but what really freaked them out was when I would not throw away a food wrapper after I had eaten its contents.

'What are you doing holding that? Throw it away!'

'No, I am going to put it in a bin.'

Astonished disbelief: 'But you've finished it! Just throw it away!'

'I don't mind. I'll just wait until we go past a bin.'

'Are you telling me you are going to carry it around all day like that?'

And so on. But I still could not throw it away. If I could not throw it away at the base, I now couldn't throw it away outside the base.

A life-changing thing that happened to me at that time was that I got married. This was not a love match but arranged by my father. Even though I was only 21, he thought that as his eldest son I should be married. I fought against it. It seemed to be so against his way of thinking. Perhaps there are traditions that are so ingrained that even a man as thoughtful and liberal as my father couldn't go against them. A match was arranged, and I got married. Poor girl. I was far too young for this, and I was largely absent. I would be away for months at a time, and she lived with my parents. Every so often I would be back in Kabul for a few days to be with her, but even then I was working so would only really be at home for 6 or 7 hours a day. To make matters worse we started a family almost immediately. Oddly enough my father never arranged a marriage for any other of his children. Even my sisters, who as time went on would in turn tell him who they wanted to marry, he told them it was fine.

I was steadily promoted, and given greater and greater responsibility until I found myself head of all the 'terps' at COIN. One of the colonels who was working as an operation commander of that academy chose me to be his linguist. I really enjoyed working with him. A trust built up between us. But the fact that he gave me some responsibility caused problems with the Colonel's subordinates, who resented the Afghan terp with greater access than them.

A Captain, who could speak Farsi but was the most incompetent, childish officer I ever came across, couldn't take criticism and thought he knew everything. This resentment bubbled to the surface in 2009 when the Colonel went on leave. I had an argument with the Captain, who was temporarily in charge, about his access to certain files. The Captain blew it up out of all proportion and accused me of being a Taliban spy and that I would wear a suicide vest to blow Americans up. In my fury I made some unwise remarks to him that, at the very least, amounted to insubordination. The Captain was not universally liked or admired, but nonetheless I was suspended for six months. I was told to lie low, and I would get my old job back after the inevitable investigation once the Colonel had returned. What shocked me was that the rest of the people working with the academy were naive enough to believe him. It showed how the screening system and background checks were weak and biased in this academy.

I was devastated. I had lost the job I loved, and there was no certainty I would get it back again. I had, however, saved quite a lot of money from my generous pay. Some friends of mine who lived in Dubai persuaded me to go and stay with them for a while. I stuck it out for about a month but found life there boring and meaningless. I missed Kabul and missed having a sense of purpose, so I returned to wait out my suspension and hoped to resume my career at COIN, if they would have me back. But how was I going to pass the time? I had no idea that the next step of my life would be the best years of my life.

One day when I was mooching about at my cousin's house, he said to me, 'Have you heard? The British are looking for interpreters? You should work for them until you're allowed to go back to the Americans. They pay good money, and it'll be something to do.' I took his advice and went to Camp Souter the next day with my CV.

Chapter 8

The Queen's Shilling – *Khedmat ba Malika*

The gap between an army and the foreign country in which it operates is fertile ground for entrepreneurs, idealists, spies and black marketeers. An army without interpreters is blind and deaf.

When the coalition forces swept the Taliban from power, there was no home army, no police, no government and no institutions to which they could attach themselves for support, only the Northern Alliance and the armies of the warlords. So the coalition armies paid very good money to find men who would bridge the gap, and let them see, feel and hear.

Of course it is a very dangerous job, especially in a country that traditionally has no love for any foreign army on its soil. The high level of compensation available to interpreters attracts the bad as well as the good, and some pretty rank weeds take root in the crevices between the foreign army and the native population.

Raffi was head of the interpreters at Camp Souter, and he controlled the interface between the British and Afghans. I handed him my CV. He looked it over and said to me: 'Sure you can join, this is a great CV. You have to pass some tests, but that won't be a problem.' I told him that I was keen to start as soon as possible. 'Great,' he replied, 'I will process your CV. If you don't get in it's free, but you have to pay me your first month's salary if you are accepted.'

A cold feeling went down my spine. I told him, 'I don't need to pay you, and I don't need the job.' I didn't know it but our brief and heated exchange was noticed by a passing officer. As I was leaving he came up to me and asked why I was there. I told him I was applying to be an interpreter. The officer told me to come back the next day and he would personally meet me at the gate. Many of the applicants standing there could not speak fluent English, but I had no difficulties and he noticed that.

I turned up the next day, expecting very little. I was met by the officer, who asked for my CV. I handed it to him and left. Normally there was a two or three week wait for an interview, but I was called back in a couple of days. As I walked through the gates I was met by the same officer. I could see Raffi lurking in the background, furious that I had sidestepped him.

The officer asked me a few questions and then asked if I would like to sit the interpreter's test straightaway. I took the first test, which was for an entry-level job. I passed with flying colours. The officer said, 'Well you did well in that, would you like to try the next level?' I did. Again I passed with full marks. I was encouraged to try level three, which would mean a better job and better pay. I sat it and was told that I had got full marks yet again. The officer was impressed and said that it would be foolish not to try the level 4, the highest exam. This would mean one of the top jobs and a much higher pay grade. This test I passed with 73 points out of a possible 80. The officer congratulated me and told me to turn up the next day for the standard polygraph test that all interpreters needed to pass.

When I came back the next day, Raffi tried to intercept me. He was incandescent with rage, but I ignored him. The same officer met me and asked me if I was ready to go: there was one team that needed me to start right away.

'What about the polygraph?' I asked.

'Oh don't worry about that, you can do it in Helmand,' he replied, 'but are you ready to go?'

'I am ready to get back to work,' I said.

The officer said to me, 'I want to tell you something but you cannot tell anyone about it: you will be working for a team from the SAS. They're British special forces.'

'I know who the SAS are. And they want me?'

'Yes. Right away. Are you on for that?'

'Yes Sir. Yes I am.'

I was in a state of stupefaction. This was an amazing opportunity. To work for the world's best and most glorious Special Forces. It would be a huge honour to work with such a team.

The next night I was on a Chinook helicopter heading for Lashkar Gah, the British base in Helmand. When I arrived, I was met by one of the guys I would be working for. The polygraph test was never mentioned again, and I was introduced to the team. I would never return to the American army. Instead began the most intense and best time of my life.

Chapter 9

The Regiment – *Leywae Khaas*

I f it felt like I had my dream job working for the Americans, with the SAS it was as if I had suddenly discovered my purpose in life. Maybe it was by design, or chance, that the polygraph test was never mentioned again. It may have been because they knew all about me already, and knew I would be the right man for them. Or it could have been a way to show that they trusted me. Trust bestowed in this way is one of the great bonds.

That is not to say that it was easy to fit in. There is always a dickhead somewhere. And the great sport of dickheads is to go for the new boy. It is the manner in which it deals with the problem that is the mark of a great institution.

Not long after I joined I had an altercation with a member of the team over something trivial – a blanket, for God's sakes! – the idea being to goad me until I did something stupid. This duly happened, though it was hardly my fault. I had a mild tussle with the guy, not much in itself, but for an interpreter, where so much relies on judgement, and for an outsider, who should not be fighting with any of the men I was working with, it spelled trouble and was duly investigated.

I immediately feared that my fantasy job was over before it started, but I was to be pleasantly surprised. When I had got into trouble in the American army no great efforts were expended to investigate the true cause of events. This time, however, the officer commanding the team took time to find out what had really happened and why.

He interviewed me, refused to accept my resignation, and told me to go to my quarters while he looked into matters. After an intense investigation, the true state of affairs was plain. The officer apologised to me, and I was accepted back into the team. This sense of fair play impressed me deeply: I was not just an expendable local man. They had judged the case impartially and on its merits.

After that I was determined to be able to keep up with the team in all situations. This meant going on all the gruelling training exercises they provided to the Afghan special forces. Many interpreters didn't bother too much with their fitness, but for me it was an honour as well as a duty. After all, I hadn't joined just to interpret: I had joined to fight.

On one exhausting five-hour march in full kit through soft sand, the sergeant major asked me, 'Why aren't you tired?' I replied: 'Because I'm marching with you guys.'

Most of my work was at the base, translating between the SAS and Afghan intelligence services, NDS or National Directorate of Security officers and men, particularly during briefings. It was as hard going from Afghan to English as it was the other way. There was an Afghan officer at Lashkar Gah who was a nightmare for interpreters. There were times during a briefing when he would speak for 5 or even 10 minutes, which is incredibly difficult to translate. When he finished his speech, everyone would look to me to translate, keen to hear what he had said, with his commanding manner and dramatic arm movements. Then suddenly he would change his mind and say, 'Don't tell them this!' or 'Don't translate what I just said.'

I would say, 'But I can't just say nothing!' to which he would reply, 'Just make something up.' He was so unprofessional it drove me crazy. I had to explain to him many times that when he talked the British expected me to translate. 'I cannot just make stuff up!' However, the next time he would be exactly the same. He became a standing joke among all the interpreters.

Eventually I became the only non-operational man to do a parachute jump with the SAS. Now, I was ready.

Chapter 10

Covert Operations from Lashkar Gah –
Amaliat Hay Mahram az Lash Kargah

I went on roughly thirty operations from Lashkar Gah during the three or four months I was there, and they were all high-value ops: the SAS were never used on ordinary targets. Every operation was planned after weeks, or months, of preparation, intelligence gathering, and so on. Special operations were never conducted based on one intelligence, rather they were conducted when everyone was 100 per cent sure of the authenticity of the intelligence. Many in the Afghan and western media sometimes dispute this, but special operations were always based on intelligence, confirmed by many sources, including the technology available to the special operations community.

There was one operation, in 2011, that haunts me to this day. As usual it was a mission to capture or kill (if he didn't come quietly) an important Taliban commander in Sangin, a town in Helmand province in central Afghanistan. He was also mayor of the Sangin district, which shows how embedded in the local population the Taliban could be, though this didn't mean that all the local people supported the Taliban. Such figures were feared due to their influence and they had ears everywhere.

The team had intelligence that the Taliban commander was going to a mosque in a village near to Sangin. We boarded the Chinooks and headed off.

We landed around 9 pm a few kilometres away from the village so that the helicopters would not be heard and walked for three hours to get to the target. These walks weren't always easy. Usually we had to walk over a mountain to get to a target. This one was on an uneven surface through hilly terrain, with gravel. Not only had we to overcome the challenge of rough Afghan terrain, we also had to be in a state of full awareness, and, scanning our surrounding areas, making sure there were no Taliban around us, we had to be super silent. I had the responsibility to make sure that the SAS were communicating with the Afghan forces, keeping them updated, and at the same time listening to the Taliban conversation and making sure to pass it on if they talked about us or possible threats. Not only that, we also had to carry loads of gear. This could include blood (enough for everyone in case of casualty), ladders, and other equipment. It wasn't that bad in the winter, because the heavier you were, the warmer you would be, and we didn't have to worry about the cold. But in the summer it was very uncomfortable. We were basically sweating from the moment we landed from the helicopters all the way to target point. On many occasions I wouldn't wear my body armour – stupid decision now that I think about it, but at the time, in the summer and in that southern Afghanistan heat which sometimes rose to 45 Celsius or more, it made sense to go as light as possible. However, it got me in trouble with the sergeant major a few times.

As we got closer to the target, our senses were awake, adrenaline was there, and we were on high alert. The areas we operated weren't like Kabul city centre where you get a few NATO-friendly people; this was right in the middle of enemy strongholds, places where the regular army would find it impossible to go, as almost everyone was in support of the terrorist Taliban. So not only had we to make sure that the enemy wouldn't hear us, but we also had to make sure that the people living in the area didn't see us, as this would give our position away and ruin the element of surprise. Of course, technology always helps! We nearly always had the advantage of technology. When we got to the target and got into our positions, the area of operations was completely in our control. My jobs there were to communicate with the British officer and the Afghan officer, and to scan and listen to the enemy's conversation, making sure they were unaware of our location. If there were any developments, I had to pass on the information to the commanders of the British and Afghan forces so that the team was aware of the situation. In one ear I had to listen to the enemy, in the other I had a headphone to communicate with the Afghan officers and send any commands to them, making sure there were no misunderstandings. As we approached the target, I had one more responsibility: now I had to go with the assault team to conduct a call-out, to separate the women from the men to save them from harm, and give the enemy a chance to surrender to save a firefight. This was the most dangerous of all my responsibilities: since I was calling out loud, it would give away my position. To do a call-out best, I always made sure to see what was going on. Even in the dark they would hear me and easily know where the voice was coming from, and to kill an interpreter was gold to them. They knew that killing an interpreter would leave the forces deaf and blind.

At every call-out I felt it was my responsibility to make sure that the innocent lived and Taliban died. I always hoped that we would not take any terrorist Taliban alive. There was no point in taking them alive. Arresting them would mean they would go through a corrupt Afghan judicial system and the end result was almost always that they were released. Then the terrorist was back on the street to kill more British soldiers or innocent women and children. Killing was the best option; it always made me feel great to see them die.

As I conducted the call-out, and the team cleared the compound, they shot at us. Since it was a Taliban compound, no terrorist gave up. That meant one thing: death was coming to visit them that night! We were their death and they would go to hell. I was happy in their death, knowing that hundreds of innocent civilians' lives would be saved.

The Taliban never dared to target the military. Almost all of their operations were cowardly killing of innocent men, women and children. They would not stop at any age of children; they would kill toddlers, pregnant women, old men, the deaf, the blind, and so on. Just recently in 2020 they attacked a maternity clinic killings dozens of pregnant women, women who had just given birth, and babies who were one hour or one day old. Therefore, I was always pleased to see them get killed.

As the call-out failed, it was time for the assault team to do what they do best: enter the compound, kill all the armed terrorist Taliban, and clear the area. The busiest time for me was after killing the Taliban. Not only had I to carry on listening and communicating, I had to separate the women and children from other detainees and question them to get further intelligence. I also had to search paperwork and be sure to collect all the papers which could be valuable for information. At this time of the operation, my colleagues described me as a Tasmanian Devil! Meaning I was running around taking care of multiple tasks at the same time. It wasn't just me; it was the other interpreters in the operation as well – and we enjoyed it.

I never believed I did enough. I always believed that I could do more to help the team. I had to keep my wits about me at all times as I was the ears of the unit, and it was to me that the first countermoves of the Taliban would be made known. I knew that my job was very important and I had to do it well so we could have a successful operation, even though, even on my busiest night, I wouldn't have done half of what the other soldiers were doing. Despite that, our job was important. It was just to translate papers, but as a member of the team, we felt responsible to do as much as possible. Nobody told me to do all this: I worked as hard and well as I possibly could because I wanted to. What motivated us was the 'Cause' – the cause to fight terrorists, the cause to bring peace to our country.

I soon heard radio chatter from the Taliban that they had heard the commotion in Sangin and were going to engage the attackers. This they duly did, attacking the compounds that had been cleared.

After a desultory gun battle, the Chinooks arrived to take us away, but due to incoming fire they could not lift us and had to take off again. The enemy, however, did not know that we were still there. On their radios I heard them saying that they thought we were all gone. I told my commanding officer about it, and we decided to use this opportunity to ambush them. Since this was about a high-ranking commander of the Taliban, every possible step was a necessity.

We now waited in the dark for the mullah of the local mosque. We knew that the call to prayer was a code to tell the local commander that it was all clear and he could come to the village. I could hear from the radio chatter that someone close by was telling the mullah to go and make the call.

I hid just by the mosque in an alley with a couple of SAS troopers. As soon as the mullah got to the mosque door, we grabbed him, telling him not to make any noise otherwise he would be shot. After a short questioning session, I told the mullah to make the call as normal. If he said anything different to the normal call, he would be shot. The mullah, although hesitant and scared, nodded agreement and I took him to the mosque and handed him to a soldier to make his call. I went back into the street to listen to the call. It was fine.

I was just about to go back into the mosque when a group of Taliban, including the local commander, appeared in the alley. The commander was in the middle, a typical chubby Taliban commander with a big turban, two bodyguards on the left and two on the right. One had an RPG and the other three had AKs. They had obviously been hiding very close by. Because I was only stepping out to hear the Imam, I had left my gear including my body armour in the mosque, against all standards and practice. I did not expect them to get through our cordons, but this group was in one of the compounds within our cordons.

I froze, certain that this was it: I was going to die in Sangin. I had five Taliban, hardcore Taliban, armed, right in front of me. They were literally five metres away from me. Surprisingly, they froze as well; presumably I was as nasty a surprise for them as they were for me. They stared at me and I stared at them. In this very short amount of time, I saw my life in a flash! I have been close to death on numerous occasions, but this time it was different. I was standing, with my night-vision goggles, multicam uniform and no weapon. I wondered how they had passed our cordons. How did no-one see them? They were heavily armed, not that it mattered, but anyone who moved close to our area of operation would normally get shot in the face! For them, they must have thought, what the hell is this guy doing? If I was them, I would have been happy to see me, as the Taliban always loved shooting or cutting off the head of an interpreter and filming it so they could all see it.

I remember that moment very clearly to this day. If I was good at drawing, I would draw them right now! It was a green zone, meaning there were trees everywhere. In that brief moment, which didn't last more than 3–5 seconds, I saw my son, my father, my mother and siblings, I saw my childhood, being a refugee, and the whole journey. I don't how my brain processed all that, maybe it assumed this was it. I was done. I literally waited for them to shoot me. With what I thought would be my last breath I shouted, 'Weapons seen!' This is standard when fighting the Taliban, in order not to kill unarmed civilians. At least I could give the rest of the team a warning before I died. There was no point in dying quietly and letting these terrorists hurt the rest of my team mates. But, to my astonishment, it worked in quite another way. They dropped their weapons and scattered!

The others from the team quickly assembled from behind a wall in the next-door house where they were hiding. They found me traumatized.

But there was no time to moan. I just had to get my shit together and carry on with my responsibilities.

That was not the only time I came close to death. Once we were in a similar village in Helmand province and I was calling out on a number of terrorists hiding inside a mosque, including two suicide attackers. This was towards the end of my career, and we were giving more of role to the Afghan special forces, to prepare them to face the threat and be ready to take over.

As we approached the mosque, the sergeant major asked me to conduct my call-out and see if they would come out, although we knew that these terrorists were not $10 Taliban but hardcore ones, the ones who will never give up and will die fighting. I crept up close with the sergeant major and could see with my night-vision goggles the two men through a crack in the door. I called to them to come out. Usually when I started to call out I could hear a voice or something before they came out, but this time all I could hear was people moving around, perhaps preparing to counter our attack. This mosque had only one door and one window, and it was a fairly big one. According to the rules, foreign forces were not allowed to enter a mosque; only Afghan forces could and these terrorist Taliban knew that. As I was calling them out, a grenade was thrown at me in reply. I did not see the grenade, although I knew they were aware of my location and I would be the first for them to target. One of the team members saw it and yelled, 'Grenade!!' In the blink of an eye the SAS sergeant major and two more troopers who were at the gate threw themselves in front of me and shielded me from the blast. One was injured. I was in a state of shock, and the sergeant major and the uninjured soldier carried me quickly to shelter.

After a good firefight, it was time for Afghan special forces to enter the compound and take care of the terrorists. They didn't disappoint: six entered, killing all six terrorists successfully.

Once the building was clear I went to see the compound, and as I entered I saw the two suicide bombers. One had managed to blow himself up: I could only see a hand, a leg and his head – there was no sign of his other body parts. The other was at the far end of the mosque and had failed to detonate himself. Two of the goofy terrorists hid under a blanket!! The two geniuses thought it was a magic blanket and that the bullets wouldn't go through it to kill them. It felt good to see these dirty terrorist Taliban get killed before they killed innocent people.

Actions like that, or when they stood up for me on other occasions, motivated me to work harder and be even more loyal to my comrades. I felt like a member of the team because I was treated as such. Those close calls did not put me off, but I kept going until the threats got to my family.

Chapter 11

Kandahar

After Lashkar Gah, I returned to Kandahar to become part of the bigger team carrying out covert and black operations. I was given more responsibility than the other interpreters, and this task force was very active and making a massive difference in the region. Such operations were supporting my cause by eliminating terrorism from Afghanistan.

I spent a lot of time at the base with officers and men who were thoughtful and intelligent. This had happened when I was at COIN as well. By a sort of osmosis, I was picking up an attitude to life that I felt had become occluded in normal life in Afghanistan. I had begun to assume shared values such as fairness, common sense, impartial justice and belief in a civil society with strong institutions. This was more than a continuation of habits, such as standing in line, that I had learned at the American base. Though I had been given some of these values in a different form by my parents, particularly by my father, my continued association with these extraordinary men and women was changing my understanding of why I was fighting this war. It was more than just for hatred of the Taliban. A clear idea was forming of the sort of Afghanistan I was fighting for.

There were side effects to this. It was not just the constant work that was dividing me from my old friends and cousins. My immediate family might be supportive, but this was far from the case with my wider family. Many of my friends and relatives were not happy about my job. Some had become more religious as they grew up: they went around dressed in turbans, and argued vociferously with me about how I was betraying my country and religion. Others were plainly jealous of the fact that I was earning well. They could see that I had money and, without showing off, I didn't see any reason to hide it from them.

My work had also taught me to argue using reason and evidence, which was vital for operational integrity but also pleasurable in itself. But with Afghans, any argument I had using these tools would end in anger and recrimination. Emotion rather than reason ruled.

Slowly I distanced myself from those friends and relatives as surely as they removed themselves from me. My very small group of close Afghan friends comprised those to whom I could talk about what I did, although I had to be as brief as possible, as I could not share what I was actually doing.

This was not the only way that I was diverging from other Afghans. If my vision of Afghanistan was one of stability and justice, the real Afghanistan was becoming increasingly prey to corruption and cynicism.

Working at Kandahar didn't mean that I now had a desk job and was not sent on operations. Far from it: it was from Kandahar that I went on the most dangerous mission of all; one that nearly cost me and the whole team our lives: The operation in Kajaki.

This photo was taken in Panjshir Valley, the only province that was never taken by the Taliban. In the background is the home town of Ahmad Shah Massoud.

With Afghan special forces on Kandahar airfield just before an operation.

One of the best Afghan special forces operators, known for his bravery on operations.

With a US army sniper on the outskirts of Kabul.

At the American Army Counter Insurgency Academy in Kabul – Aussie and American officers.

With a group of US special forces interpreters.

With two Afghan special forces on a joint SAS/ Afghan SF operation somewhere in the desert of Helmand province. In the background are two Chinooks.

With the US special forces, in a Taliban house, during a special operation which resulted in the killing of four Taliban fighters.

This was taken at our camp in TGI Fridays on Kandahar airfield.

With an Afghan commando officer, General Waziri, who is now a well-known and very successful commando general.

With my two fellow
interpreters in 2011. Both
are now in the UK.

On a joint operation with
Afghan special forces,
Helmand province.

In the games room, just
before we went on the
Kajaki operation.

At the COIN Academy, after a lecture on Afghan culture to US and other NATO officers.

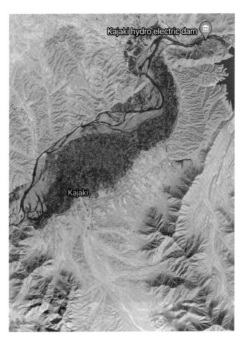

Satellite view of Kajaki – where we had that operation.

This was a patch I designed. I have one with Taliban blood on it. I rubbed it in the blood of an important target who was responsible for killing interpreters and kept it as a reminder that we take revenge.

With Afghan special forces. The plane is an RAF Tornado.

With NATO officers after completing their training on counter-insurgency in Afghanistan.

At the COIN Academy with officers from
NATO nations.

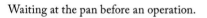

Behind me is a Tornado
which was on operations
with us.

Waiting at the pan before an operation.

A Taliban compound
about to be raided by
Afghan special forces.

A hideout where
the Taliban stored
narcotics.

Two captured Taliban
prisoners pictured in front
of confiscated cocaine.

Bonfire of the confiscated
cocaine.

Chapter 12

Kajaki

Our team was situated in a little base within the big Kandahar base. Not even regular army was allowed there; only those who worked for the task forces were allowed. I was the only Afghan civilian, along with my two other Afghan interpreters, with clearance to live there. It was a small base within a base; that's how all special forces worked: they usually had their small base within a bigger regular army base. Due to the secrecy of their operations, others were allowed in only under escort.

Late one afternoon I was honing my pool skills in the American games room, which was far more lavish than the British one. There you had several large comfortable sofas, several screens showing American football, country music in the background, and play stations everywhere, mostly featuring *Call of Duty* as I remember. I was practising for one of the endless competitions the Americans were always setting up, and my game needed a bit of improvement. Soon American soldiers were beginning to trickle in after the day's work and by about 7 o'clock the place was rammed. As soon as we started to get down to some serious pool playing, or enjoy a meal, my pager went off. This was not unusual: night time was when I often went to work. The message read, 'Orders 20:00'. I apologized to the guy I was playing with and headed to the Operations Room.

The fact that I had been called by pager meant that the operation was only minutes away. It was a moonless night, so something was always on the cards. I jumped into my car (we drove everywhere on the base, it was so huge), a Ford Ranger painted green, it looked a bit like an Afghan police car. One of the guys had a Toyota Landcruiser (which was the best, let's be honest) confiscated from a smuggler. I told my Afghan National Army liaison to text his guys to get to the pan (helicopter pad) immediately. He texted them, 'Standby'.

In the Operations Room the usual strong coffee was on the brew. Only SAS were allowed into the cool air-conditioned room with its big screens showing updated drone footage and digital maps bearing the legend 'UKSF eyes only'. I'm the only terp there; the only other Afghan there is the Afghan police special forces team commander. The door closes behind me as Sergeant Major Bob (not his real name) stands up to give the briefing, with Lieutenant J looking on.

An intercepted coded message had revealed that one of the Quetta Shura's key commanders was in Afghanistan. The Taliban high command was located in Quetta, under the protection of the Pakistani Intelligence Service, ISI. From there they directed the insurrection, via couriers and other cryptic channels of communication.

Sometimes, though, they had to make their way onto the battlefield, to inspect their junior commanders, and to relay orders that were too complicated or secret to leave to others. Most of these high-ranking commanders were Pakistanis, either Pakistani military or ISI.

This Key Commander was staying the night in Kajaki with the local commander there. We looked at the map. Kajaki was a majority pro-Taliban area in Helmand province, deep in the heart of Taliban country; a long green valley bottom, spreading below the huge Kajaki Dam. The hills were ours, sort of, but the valley was completely under the insurgents' control. I glanced at Garry (not his real name), my fellow interpreter, who would also be coming with us. He raised an eyebrow apprehensively and grinned. I looked around and everyone in the room was smiling, keyed up and bursting with contained excitement. We were going out on an Op, and a big Op. That was typical of the SAS: the more dangerous the operation, the more excited they would be. This excitement and high morale always made me feel safe. There was no better team to go to such dangerous places than the glorious British SAS.

Back to the briefing: One of the guys was Irish, and one of the officers would sometimes wind him up by asking me to translate what he said. The banter was always on between them, but he was professional to his fingertips. Lieutenant Jones was young, very knowledgeable, and very posh! – from one of the grander British regiments. He was not just well spoken, but polite, and never swore. Handsome like a film star, the APU (Afghan Partner Unit, a special force unit) used to call him the good-looking officer or the handsome English. He was always straight down the line, but with a smile. Like all SAS officers he was politically smart. The APU officer in the briefing was Pashtun and an OK guy. He was taller than me with a bit of beard growth. I translated the briefing for him. His experience was more in the field of counter-narcotics than counter-terrorism.

The pan was ten minutes away, so we jumped in our vehicles and raced out there. The APU were not allowed to bring their mobile phones so they had to ditch them. Our group consisted of

SAS, APU and the SFSG (Special Forces Support Group) from 1 Para, who were to be the cordon for our operation. There was also the Afghan JO (Judicial Officer) who represented the state and the law. (The Afghan JOs represented the law but had no legal education; this one did not even understand basic Afghan law, he knew only about Afghan culture.)

At the pan, after briefing the Afghan special forces troops, we lined up and waited for the SAS commander to give the order to move. Everyone checked their weapons and did communication checks, there was a last-minute intel report, and then a head count before we started lining up towards our Chinooks. When we were 30 or 40 metres away from them, we stopped. All the men were ready to go and get this operation done, make a difference and save lives. As we were standing, the Chinooks were turning and burning, and this beautiful sound of Chinook engines, the warm breeze hitting our faces in this warm evening was a special feeling. No word was spoken, just waiting to get a go-ahead from the pilots to make our way towards the Chinooks. No matter how tired, no matter how our morale was, this moment gave me a feeling of strength and high adrenaline. We made our way towards the specially adapted Chinooks and all crammed quickly in.

The Chinooks lifted and left the Kandahar airfield and I looked out to admire that view. Well lit up, Kandahar airfield looked like a small town; after all it was home to twenty thousand plus NATO soldiers. I wondered, will I come back alive, or is this the last time I will see this base? But this was my last thought which wasn't operation-related. After that, my brain was focused entirely on my responsibilities.

We were after a rare and golden target. The senior Taliban travelled secretly, they invariably went unarmed and with no means of identification on them. They carried no computers, no phones, no papers. Under our rules of operation, we could not hold them as they were not doing anything illegal, and under the rules of engagement set by NATO and the Afghan government, we were not allowed to shoot unless we were being shot at or a visible threat was there. The Taliban commanders at the time mostly carried no weapon. The ones who did carry a weapon would not go without a fight, so almost always they got killed in the exchange.

If we could catch one who was staying with a local commander, then we would have him bang to rights. But by doing it in Kajaki, we would be putting our hand into the hornets' nest, or not just our hands, this was like climbing into a hornets' nest the size of a town – and where it was almost impossible for a coalition forces vehicle to come or helicopters to land.

The Kajaki Dam is well known because of two famous actions there. Not long before, it had been in the hands of ISAF (the NATO-led International Security Assistance Force) and the ANA (Afghan National Army). Its waters feed the green valley floor below. But now there was no ISAF presence there: it was completely under the control of the Taliban. The Key Commander presumably imagined himself safe there. If something went wrong with this mission, there would be no cordon of friendly outposts and nowhere from which rescuing sorties might be made. In Kajaki we would be on our own, surrounded by hardcore Taliban terrorists who would love to die fighting and killing us.

Somewhere out in the dark air, shadowing the Chinooks, was a specially adapted C130 air support gunship festooned with guns, rockets and bombs. It had the capacity to interfere with the enemy's ground communications. And it could launch drones as well. If things got really bad, we could call up Tornadoes and Apache helicopters (although when the terrain is green zone, even Apaches would be blind and could do little to help us).

Forty-odd of us sat inside the Chinooks, on two facing benches with the SFPG and APU guys sitting on the floor. We were in complete darkness as no chink of light could be allowed. The night's cool air blew through the chopper from the gun ports. The only smell was fuel, and the occasional fart.

After an hour in the air the pilot gave us the ten-minute warning. I checked my equipment and put on my night-vision goggles. Five minutes from the target the Chinooks swooped down low to fly in at ground level to give the enemy the hardest target possible. My stomach dropped with the chopper. The two-minute call felt like twenty seconds, then came the one-minute warning. The warning was usually called by the commander of the squadron and I was passing it on loud in English and Dari for the Afghan special forces to prepare themselves. We heard AK47s popping off from the ground. The door gunners returned fire. Everyone tensed for action. We held tight till we came to a dead stop. The rear door was already open. The landing was a bit rough and then we were piling out, SAS assault team first. The sergeant major and I were out last. We had only a few seconds to deploy before the Chinooks took off again. They were not landing for long, they were supposed to just touch down, we had to run and get off the helicopter as soon as possible for them to fly back out. By the time I got out the assault team was already engaging the enemy.

As I hit the ground, I immediately smelt that burnt cow-shit smell of the countryside – this was typical Helmand – and a fresh, after-rain odour.

We had landed beside the two compounds that were our target. I was engulfed by a maelstrom of dust and straw whipped up into a tornado by the rotors, gritting my mouth and nose and plastering my goggles. I staggered through the cloud of chaff. It was hard to see anything. I glimpsed the blurry figure of the sergeant major running towards the closest of the compounds and sprinted after him. I don't know why, but as the Chinooks took off I had a feeling in my gut that it was going to be a long night.

Within twenty seconds of landing I was inside the compound. Through my radio I heard Taliban chatter saying, 'The green-eyed devils are here!' A battle was raging, but without night vision the Taliban were at a fatal disadvantage. The Taliban did own night-vision goggles, but only their high-valued commanders or their watchmen got to use them. Unfortunately nowadays they have access to night-vision goggles in almost all provinces and at even lower level insurgency; they have managed to capture many from Afghan forces. The assault team was way too fast for them. I saw a couple of Taliban killed as they tried to counter-attack; I guess they had no idea who they were facing. The battle was over in two minutes. Very rarely could the Taliban fight the SAS for longer than five minutes. In the compound yard I stepped over two dead Taliban who had been dispatched with a classic 'double tap' to the head. Their face shape was changed, eyes popped out, some brains on the side of their heads, and they had their chest rig and weapons on them. There were six dead altogether, including the local commander, who had been fighting with his pistol. He had been playing host to his Quetta-based superior.

I pushed aside the heavy blanket that served as a door to keep the cool night air out, and entered the building. With no windows, the stuffy air inside was thick with the hum of man and beast: that cattle shit smell that seems to have been sweated into the fabric of the building, cut with the odour of sleeping bodies – these country insurgents rarely wash more than weekly, and seldom brush their teeth.

Only one insurgent was left alive: the Key Commander from the Quetta Shura, who sat glowering in the main room, held at gunpoint by a man from the assault team. Other members of the team were already undertaking the Search and Seek for Evidence, or SSE for short. They rifled through the meagerly furnished rooms for mobile phones, USB sticks, computers, paperwork, training literature, anything that might give us information about the operational capacity, planning, equipment and training of our enemy.

Usually in other operations my first job would be to take care of the women and children, gathering them into one room and assuring them that no harm would come to them. Usually women and children would make a hell of a drama! So it was important to calm them down. Here, however, there were none. Nor were there any livestock in the open area of the compound. This was a terrorist base, not a home. I looked round the room. It was absolutely typical: there was nothing out of the ordinary here, just the usual plastic matting, cheap home-made mattresses, a couple of religious posters and a bare alcove in the wall.

The sergeant major and I looked down at the key commander. The sergeant major tore off the hat the man had hurriedly crammed on his head. He was chubby and of medium height, with a round Helmandi face, small nose, full cheeks and brown eyes. His hair was cut short straight across his forehead and his beard was neatly groomed. He was noticeably cleaner than his hosts, though his clothes, the brown dishdash and Nike slippers typical in Helmand, were dirtier than they probably were normally after his sojourn in the field. About 35–40 years old, he represented the new generation in the Taliban high command.

He looked at the ground, conserving energy for what was coming. Sergeant Major Bob leant forward and took the prisoner firmly by the arm. He lifted him up, turning to me and saying, 'Let's take him somewhere quiet.'

I nodded as he propelled the commander out through the doorway.

Now my job had really begun. I already had in one ear a radio tuned to the Afghan National Army frequency and in the other, one tuned to the Taliban frequency. In addition to that I now had to translate for the sergeant major in a vital preliminary interrogation of the prisoner.

Next door was a storage room with boxes and a filing cabinet. We pushed the Taliban commander into it and sat him on a box. I perched on the filing cabinet, and the sergeant major on another box. A minute later the Afghan Judicial Officer came in. He looked round momentarily for somewhere to sit. The sergeant major stuck a leg out, shoving a box the JO's way. He nodded thanks at the sergeant major and with a small glance at me sat down. Now the interrogation could begin. The role of the Judicial Officer is to report to the Afghan government, and he is supposed to be a guarantee of proper conduct towards the detainees and to stand witness in court. He also shared any intelligence gathered from the Taliban commander with his superiors.

This JO was a Pashtun from Eastern Afghanistan; they were traditionally more liberal than the southern Afghan ones. I had heard that he had a lot of enemies in his village thanks to family feuds and had been shot a few times. He was five foot seven, clean shaven, very tough and very fit. He was 38 but had never been promoted past the rank of sergeant thanks to a hopeless hashish addiction that made him a bit crazy, or at least not all there. Mind you, being shot in the head wouldn't have helped. He always had a smile on his face, he was always up for laughs and, as I said before, had no special knowledge of the law that I could discern.

He had been either from the first or maybe the second batch of recruits to the APU. The first and second recruits received training directly from the British special forces and were the best of that unit, especially Khushal, who later at 35 years old became a famous general in Afghanistan. Unlike most Pashto (even within the ANA) he loathed the Taliban. The APU was not a military outfit but a police counter-terrorist unit operating under the Ministry of the Interior. This was a legacy of the UK's counter-narcotic role in Afghanistan, which meant that we had gone to the police rather than the ANA to form this unit.

'What's your name?' asked the sergeant major to our captive. I translated.

'Imran Khan [not his real name].'

We looked at each other. I had not expected a Taliban to give his true name.

'Age?'

'I don't know.'

'Occupation?'

'Farmer.'

I scarcely needed to translate that. Everyone in Afghanistan is a farmer, and so is every Taliban when asked.

The sergeant major stood up, looking down on the Taliban who returned his stare with defiance. I stood as well. I had to interpret the sergeant major's body language as well as the tone of his voice. British and Afghan body language is very different, so to give the Afghan the full import of the sergeant major's questions, I had to translate even the way the soldier stood.

Just as the sergeant major opened his mouth to speak, I heard a blast of radio chatter in my 'Taliban' ear. I held up my hand and the words died on his lips. Ever since we landed I had been listening to the enemy. On the radio I heard an endless stream of old-fashioned greetings, followed by a lot of talk about mysterious helicopters and gunfire. Now it was all quiet. We wondered why. More Taliban joined the conversation. Some said they had heard gunfire. Theories flew about. Then one voice, speaking softly, talked about the firefight:

'They are here,' said one.

'What are they doing?' asked another.

'They attacked the local commander's house.' Pause. 'They are there now.'

All eyes were fixed on me. I listened to the quiet one. He was speaking softly because he was near. He was talking about 'here', which could only mean he was in one of the five compounds that made up the hamlet. I turned to the sergeant major.

'They're here. And they know we're here.'

'How close?'

'One of them is very close.'

'Right. Time to go.'

He pulled the Taliban commander upright from his box and pushed him firmly through the door.

'Time to go lads!' the sergeant major shouted. Lieutenant Jones appeared with Garry, my fellow 'terp', who had been listening to the same chatter.

'We've been spotted,' he said. He spoke quietly to the sergeant major, who then turned to two SAS troopers.

'With me.'

He nodded to me, and the four of us walked out into the compound's garden. Around us men were getting ready to leave. We crept swiftly to the entrance and slipped out. I walked behind the sergeant major as we moved down an alley between the two compounds. When we got to the end there was a small irrigation ditch, and a single building without a compound, which was unremarkable apart from sprouting a tall pole with blue loudspeakers strapped to the top of it to call the faithful to prayer.

We all stopped and listened. I was certain that the Taliban radio man was in the mosque. I tapped Sergeant Major Bob's shoulder, pointing at the building. We moved towards it. There was a little bridge over the watercourse, but we didn't use it. We never used those bridges: they are the best places to put IEDs. Instead we slipped noiselessly down the bank and waded through the metre-deep water.

The sergeant major and I approached the door. We got close enough to open it, and I was actually reaching out to the handle when there was a sharp hiss behind me. I turned and looked. Everyone was looking down to the side of the door. Through my night-vision goggles I saw wires poking out from the side. I stood very still.

'Do you see the wires?' whispered the sergeant major. I nodded and dropped a light stick that illuminated the scene through our goggles. We followed the wires from the door to the edge of the irrigation channel. They were attached to jerry cans half buried in the side of the ditch – certainly full of explosives.

The sergeant major nodded, holding his hand up in the 'stop' position to the guys behind. We backed away from the building, and made our way along the canal towards the field where we had been dropped by the Chinooks. I dropped another stick to light the way and, I hoped, to reveal any other hidden IEDs. On the other side of the ditch were the compounds, which were dark and silent. But I could hear through my earpiece in the darkness the chatter of the enemy. They were wide awake.

It was 4 am when we arrived back at the local commander's compound. At 5 am it would get light. The team agreed to head out to the Extraction Point, a couple of miles away. Our prisoner was placed in the care of the APU team. There was a quiet moment to check that everything and everyone was in place and then we moved off, following two minesweepers who gingerly swept the ground in front of them. Every so often they dropped light sticks to show us the safe route to follow.

At this time of year, June and July, it was really cold just before dawn, however hot it got during the day. The sky was beautifully clear, with the stars shining, undimmed by any sort of pollution. I was tired and hungry. We had been working non-stop for over six hours, though it felt like it had all happened in the space of half an hour. It would take us forty-five painful minutes, going carefully, to cover the two miles to the extraction zone. Second by second we were approaching dawn, when we would no longer have the advantage of the darkness. Soon the horizon greyed, the light seeping in around us and the landscape slowly becoming visible. Kajaki is green and beautiful and in the clear air one can see for miles.

We could hear movement in the compounds at the edge of the field, and smell the first fires being lit. In my ear was a growing

Taliban hysteria about our raid. I could hear that there were a couple of guys moving from compound to compound trying to track where we had been. Those tall blank mud walls had eyes searching for us, and soon the darkness would be gone altogether. Curiously I felt in a good mood. Dawn is always exhilarating. It's something about the air and the smell of the fresh grass.

Then I heard it. The moment one of the Taliban thought he could see us. Excitedly he was telling the others over the radio. I wasn't surprised: by now we could see each other without the aid of light sticks and green vision, becoming blurry targets as the tops of the surrounding hills coloured pale pink.

Finally we arrived at the place where we were to be picked up. It was ominously quiet. The sergeant major turned to me and said, 'Two minutes to extraction!' I passed it onto the Afghan soldiers. I felt very relieved that we would soon be out of there, because the radio chatter was by now extremely lively. The Taliban had us in their sights. I would have dearly liked to suggest an air strike to give us cover, but under the rules of engagement that sort of indiscriminate fire was completely forbidden. So we waited, as the sun crept up the other side of the hills, sitting ducks, waiting for the first shot in the emerging beauty of the lush green landscape. I could never forget that view, on one side you have muddy compounds, and on the other green fields, an irrigation ditch and more fields with trees all around them, and at the end you could see the tall mountains!

Suddenly we heard the distant *wokka-wokka* sound of approaching helicopters. Two dots were approaching, low and fast, weaving and dancing like mayflies. As they got closer the Chinooks pirouetted sideways, jinked upwards, stood on end, then darted forwards. We could hear the crackle of gunfire goading them into their crazy acrobatics, and the distant whoosh of RPGs.

Standing beside the sergeant major I could hear the pilots' request to abort the extraction because of the heavy incoming fire.

A moment later I saw two RPGs fired from the right at the Chinooks, then a rain of bullets fired towards them. There was nothing we could do. We just hoped that the RPGs would miss – and they did, just. It was a moment like you'd see in movies, but this was real!

We quickly assembled into two parallel lines ready to clamber in. As they touched down, bullets pinged off their sides and the arc of an RPG skewed off crazily into the distance.

We were engulfed in a storm of blowing dust, grit and straw. The two lines of men darted forward, but to our astonishment the Chinooks did not even open their doors. No sooner had they touched down than they were taking off again, without us. We stopped and stared as the choppers lifted, turned and headed back the way they had come, bullets striking them like angry wasps. They only had to wait fifteen seconds and we would have all been aboard! Surely it was a bluff and they would circle around and pick us up. But now they were fading away, swerving crazily through bullets and RPGs. Even more RPGs were fired at them on their way back than before they landed. As I watched, I anxiously hoped they would not hit; and with the skills of these well-trained special pilots they were able to dodge, and then they were gone. And then we, as a small team, had to deal with thousands of Taliban in their stronghold, in the sunny, hot Kajaki.

As the last bits of dust and straw settled back to earth, we stayed kneeling in our two lines, looking at each other. We were totally exposed now. Nobody said anything, but they didn't need to: everyone's eyes screamed, 'What the fuck are we going to do now?' Lieutenant Jones cleared his throat, looked at a map and said, in his most imperturbable manner, 'Yes, well, obviously that's a bit disappointing.'

The commanders gathered around and immediately decided to make a move. It was not safe to stay in position, in this exposed field as we were. We all knew that it was not the pilots' fault; in fact if anything these pilots risked their lives to make sure we were not on board so we didn't get shot down. One RPG could have been another Operation Red Wings Chinook tragedy, in which a Taliban RPG shot down a helicopter killing sixteen Navy Seals and Special Forces aviators. It was a good decision to leave us behind; it gave us a better chance. It is the British army's worst nightmare when their valuable Special Forces operatives die in a helicopter crash, and not only one but one squadron!

We had to get out of the bottom of the valley. There was no way a Chinook could expect to get us out of these flat fields with gunmen hiding in every compound, tree line and ditch. I looked at the map. It was not actually that far to the bare hills at the sides of the valley, where with a little luck a Chinook would be able to land and take off. If we stayed in the main irrigation ditch, it would take us to the flat green edge of the valley. From our position, the ditch led away from the field for a few hundred metres before curving in a rough arc towards a village. Beyond the village the dusty hills rose up to a desert plateau.

Everyone hoped that the Chinooks' manoeuvre might have fooled the Taliban into thinking that we had been extracted, and that we might be able to make our way out unnoticed. But I could hear from the chatter that the enemy was wise to this and had been counting the seconds. The Taliban did not believe for a moment that there had been enough time for the team to be lifted out. In fact some of the locals were reporting that they could see us in the open field, and not long after that they started shooting at us.

We needed to get to cover quickly. As though they were reading our thoughts, a heavy machine gun opened fire on us. We dashed for the main irrigation canal, plunging into the water which came over my waist. The water was cold, and the lip of the ditch wasn't much higher than the level of the water. We settled into a wet crouch. The side of the ditch was muddy with the odd tree root sticking out. Underfoot the oozing mud at the bottom of the channel sucked at our boots. There were frogs everywhere. Our world had shrunk to a two-metre wide horizon.

But my world was the airwaves. In my other ear the Operations Room at Kandahar was swinging into frenetic action. Air cover was being scrambled and sent to Kajaki. The enemy was busy too. Taliban reinforcements from miles around were jumping into their cars to join the fun. I could even hear them tuning in from Sangin, about fifty miles away, or three to four hours' drive, pleading with the local Taliban to keep the infidel soldiers pinned down until 9 am when they would arrive. I relayed this to the sergeant major who replied cheerfully: 'Nine o'clock? We'll be long gone by then, Eddie!'

We moved off, and as the team started to wade slowly through the water of the ditch, partially hidden by scrubby grass, it quickly became apparent that progress was going to be very slow indeed. Each step was an intense effort thanks to the mud. Luckily the end of the valley did not look too far away – on the map.

Initially the ditch ran parallel to an open field to our right. On the far side of this field were two compounds.

Suddenly bullets cracked overhead. Another heavy machine gun had opened up from one of the compounds. We crouched lower in the water.

The sergeant major and I edged up to the lip of the ditch and peered over. It was impossible to see which compound the gunfire was coming from. The Taliban shooter must be deep inside it, as we could see no sign of muzzle flash or dust.

We ducked back down into the ditch and made our way forward with relentless fire cracking over our heads. On Radio Taliban I heard that they were putting a couple of mortars into place. Down in the ditch, we were nearing a looping left-hand bend. The plan was to cut the corner and make a run for it to the safety of the ditch further on, thereby avoiding being enfiladed as the ditch curved, and also saving a lot of time wading through the thick muddy water. But the manoeuvre was going to be impossible with this heavy machine-gun fire. And there was the imminent prospect of mortar shells raining down on us.

It was nine o'clock in the morning and we were completely pinned down. To move forward we had not only to wade through the mud, but clear the route of Taliban fighters who were firing at us from all around, and be cautious of IEDs and other threats. In four hours we had travelled only 200–250 metres.

I looked up to see our drones circling, and even a couple of Tornadoes. But they might as well have been on the moon if they didn't know which compound to attack. Then, suddenly, I got a clue from the chatter. One of the Taliban fighters was talking about the compound on his left. That meant that the fire was coming from the compound on my right. I told the sergeant major.

'Are you absolutely sure?' the sergeant major asked.

'Yes! It's the one on the right.'

The sergeant major wanted to be 100 per cent sure: he asked me how I knew it was the compound on the right?

'Because Taliban who are facing us, saying that it is on his left, me facing him is on my right,' I replied.

The sergeant major shouted the coordinates through to the Operations Room. Not before time a C130 gunship arrived and plastered the compound on the right with machine-gun fire, dust springing up from the bullets – and then demolished it with a rocket. There was a vast explosion and a mushroom of mud bricks dissolving into thick brown dust as the rocket hit. Over the radio I heard that the mortars had been destroyed. The heavy machine gun had also been silenced. The dust cloud slowly dispersed revealing that the building was still standing, thanks probably to its metre-thick walls. Taking no chances the gunship kept plastering the area with gunfire to keep any remaining Taliban pinned down.

As if by appointment I could hear over the radio that Taliban reinforcements were arriving from Sangin. I gave the sergeant major a look as if to say, 'And...?' He ignored this piece of impertinence.

Lieutenant Jones quickly divided us into four teams to make the dash to cut the corner. The first team hopped out of the ditch and ran the hundred-odd metres through the rough grass and scrub saplings back into the main irrigation ditch that ran at right-angles to its previous course. They didn't attract much fire, but were spotted.

The second team broke cover, but the enemy, having seen the manoeuvre, raked them with AK47 fire. They made the cover of the ditch with one casualty. One member of our team was wounded in the leg, not badly, and there was not much blood.

The medic gave him some morphine for the pain and mercifully he was able to walk.

I was in the third group. I scrambled up over the lip of the ditch with the rest of them. We ran for our lives through the rough grass and scrub, AK47 bullets cracking past our ears, and safely slithered into the ditch. Nobody was hurt. All that remained was for Lieutenant Jones and the fourth group to make it safely across the corner.

The Taliban were waiting for them, zeroed in on the route they would take. We could barely watch as the bullets zipped past them as they jinked through the deadly open space. Astonishingly they plopped into the water beside us without a scratch. It was a miracle that none of the team had been killed. The last man was the officer in command. This showed true leadership, the last man was usually at most risk. As the location gets more and more exposed, the risk to the last few gets higher.

This stretch of the ditch led straight towards the edge of the valley floor, and we moved off wearily through the ooze. To our left was a line of trees running alongside the ditch. To our right was an open field with another line of trees running along the far side of it. This was where hundreds of Taliban had taken cover.

At ten o'clock the temperature really started to climb. I had been numbed by the cold water to begin with, and then so focused on the enemy that I hadn't had the time to notice anything else.

From the growing Taliban radio chatter it seemed that insurgents were heading to Kajaki from all over the country. They came in cars and on motorbikes. Everyone wanted to be there for the kill. It was impossible for the drones to call down airstrikes on cars that might easily have contained innocent men, women or children. Once they were in the Kajaki valley there was no

Afghan or Western military presence to check them. They could operate in the open.

We slogged through the watery slime, with bullets ricocheting over our heads. Luckily for us the Taliban couldn't fire down into the ditch without exposing themselves. One Taliban fighter foolishly climbed a tree to get a better angle. The APU soldier next to me sharply raised his gun and dispatched the insurgent with two shots. Unfortunately he was left-handed and fired right beside my ear, momentarily deafening me so I could not hear the chatter. I could see other Taliban being shot out of the trees – they were pretty easy to hit.

My hearing returned just in time to hear the Taliban planning to ambush us in the market place up ahead. They knew what the infidel plan was, because by now it was obvious. There was only one way out. The ditch ran straight and eventually came to a village. We had to go through the village to get out of the valley.

Somewhere along the line the team had picked up a couple of extra prisoners: locals who were working in the fields. I squelched over to question them. They were both about 40–50 years old, but looked much older with deep-lined faces and beards. They wore shalwar chemise, pulled up so the bottom of their legs were bare.

I asked one of them, 'What do they mean by the market? Is it up ahead? Is it in the village?'

He just laughed at me, 'You're going to die today!'

The sergeant major shook his head. 'We've got to get more information. Try the other one.'

I asked the other the same question. He suggested that we should get out of the ditch and run across the field. He obviously wanted us to get shot down in the open; I gave him a contemptuous look, which he ignored. There was no other way to go but onwards, and deal with the market ambush when we got there.

At last we could hear the sharp, buzzy sound of a couple of Apache helicopters. Their insect-like forms swooped down low towards the tree line. We all stopped what we were doing and watched. They stopped in a hover and plastered the trees with fire before moving on.

However, the dead insurgents were soon replaced by fresh volunteers, and our respite was brief. The journey had already taken a tremendous toll on our bodies. I thought I was pretty fit and it didn't seem that we had travelled that far, but my legs were burning with pain at every sucking step.

At that time of year in Kajaki, June and July, the nights are cold but the days are incredibly hot. At noon the temperature was over 45 degrees centigrade. Most of us had run out of water. I still had some left, as well as some food in my pack, which I was saving for an emergency. I looked up at the trees. The leaves were ruffled by a tantalising breeze. If I could stand up I would feel it, and perhaps get a breath of cool air. It was so close I could touch it – at the risk of getting shot. I ripped off my shirt sleeves instead to get some relief.

All the while every tortured pace was taking us nearer the compound buildings that sat at the end of the irrigation ditch. They had to be taken before we could continue our line of march.

The first in was the assault team, the same guys who had cleared the local commander's compound last night. They did their job efficiently, and once they had finished, the sergeant major sent me forward to see if they had captured some locals and needed an interpreter.

I pushed past the assorted soldiers ahead of me, sweating to get ahead of the queue that was wading towards the compounds. Out in front I moved as fast as I could through the ooze. I had to run at a crouch as I came under fire from both left and right, bullets furrowing both sides of the ditch. I reached the end of the ditch and crawled out. Before they could zero in on me, I got up and dashed for the cover of the compounds a few yards away. I threw myself behind the wall, and bent over panting in front of the assault team. As the sergeant major had thought, they were holed up with a group of locals they had just captured. Bullets thwacked into the compound walls from all sides but the men of the SAS team were completely calm. Such was their professionalism that they seemed to be on exercise rather than in a desperate situation with only one, very risky, way out. They chatted and joked, ribbing me a bit, but their eyes were everywhere on the lookout. Their morale was always high.

The rest of the group came panting into the alley and dropped to the ground slumping against the walls. We were all exhausted – even the Paras from the SFSG seemed to be showing signs of strain. It was almost embarrassing as the Lieutenant and Sergeant Major chatted away as if they had been on a stroll. This was something I noticed about these guys: they moved in the same way, they even held their weapons the same way, and nothing could faze them, or even tire them out. There was something robotic about it, or perhaps as if they had all been cloned in some weird experiment – they were roughly all about the same size and shape. I never saw any one of them show weakness, either by word or body language.

In contrast, our prisoner didn't look in great shape, sandwiched between the APU officer and sergeant major. It must have been a nightmare for him, caught between hope and despair; as much despair as a Taliban can feel. After all, there was every chance he might be rescued, if he wasn't killed in error by his own side. The APU officer looked over to me, and looked away. We had never got on. He resented the way that I obviously only told him what I thought he needed to know and not a word more. Frankly he was a buffoon. Very tall and pale with a big nose, he hailed from northern Afghanistan, he originally served in the Northern Alliance, and he was traditionally conservative, that is to say he approved of the burka but was not above flirting with women and having a discreet drink from time to time. He was pretty stupid and laughed at the most puerile jokes, yet he was recently promoted to head of security of the eastern province of Afghanistan, Jalalabad.

Among his other irritating traits was a refusal to share his water or food with anyone. He was a fool even in his own village where he had flunked school, and his promotion to officer rank was a mystery until you realized that his uncle was an influential officer who now headed the Afghan special forces. I always suspected that his attitude towards the Taliban was rather equivocal.

The APU sergeant major on the other hand was excellent. Tough, brave and keen, he was given no chance to lead by his officer, and was destined to remain a sergeant major for the rest of his career. Clean shaven and looking like a proper soldier, he was liked and trusted by the SAS and got on well with Sergeant Major Bob, who approved of his good fitness levels (he was a taekwondo enthusiast). He loathed the Taliban and loved to have a drink with me and the SAS (and anyone else sympathetic for that matter). I watched him scowl at the prisoner, and shared a quick grin with him when he looked up at me.

I walked over to where the other detainees were sitting against a wall. They looked at me warily. I started asking them about the

Taliban positions and where the market place was, but mostly they said nothing, staring at the ground or shrugging. I wasn't expecting much. They had nothing to gain, and a lot to lose, by giving information to the infidel troops. Their captivity would be only temporary as they could plainly see that there were far too many of them to be taken wherever we were going, and there was no proof that any of them were Taliban anyway.

The last of our team made it to the compounds and took cover between the two buildings, grabbing a short respite from the gunfire. Within moments another heavy machine gun opened up on us from somewhere. We were now also being attacked with rocket propelled grenades. The lieutenant called in more air support. Over the radio I could hear the Operations Room frantically trying to find out from the drones buzzing around in the sky above us where the fire was coming from.

In my other ear I heard that the Taliban were swarming ahead of us, and closing up behind us and on both sides. By now there were hundreds of them.

By now it was mid-afternoon. We had been under near constant fire for over nine hours – and worse was to come. In front of us was a small wheat field, along the edges of which were small buildings and compounds. We needed to cross it before we got to the next cover, a small ditch leading to an alley between three or four compounds.

Again we formed into four groups to cross the open ground. I was in the second group. The first group, the assault team, rushed the two hundred metres of the field before the Taliban zeroed in. They made it without casualties.

My group burst from cover and we began to sprint across the field, the wounded team member on a stretcher. My heart was hammering and I expected to be gunned down at any moment. This time they were ready, and we hadn't gone twenty yards before we had to hit the floor, taking what little cover we could from the standing wheat. We started to crawl as bullets cracked over our heads. I immediately regretted cutting the arms off my shirt as I dragged myself through the spiky wheat stalks – suffering a thousand tiny pinpricks sticking through the sweaty grime. The incoming fire was so intense it seems a miracle that we were not all wiped out. I heard the crack and whoosh of the RPG man starting up, and an explosion in the middle of the field.

Just when it seemed that we would be pinned down forever, two Tornadoes thundered past, laying down fire on the surrounding buildings in a cacophony of shattered blocks and pluming mud. They were followed by the C130 gunship with its huge machine guns. The RPG man was silenced, but more importantly the dust raised by the gun and rocket fire provided the perfect cover for us to get up and sprint forward. We made another thirty yards before the dust settled and we had to hit the dirt again. We crawled forward until the planes returned and laid down more fire. We leapt up in unison and sprinted another thirty yards before going to ground. During this time, I was next to the commanding officer. He was not only being mindful of the lives for which he was responsible, but at the same time he was making sure his teams were moving and following according to plan. He was calm and focused, like it was just another exercise. He was one of the best officers I have ever met, the way he was leading his team was extraordinary!

Finally we cleared the field, launching ourselves into the cover of the ditch, sweating grittily and with mouths parched like sandpaper from the dust and chaff. I looked round to see that one of the group was injured. The soldier, one of the APU, had a leg wound, worse than the SAS soldier's flesh wound. He could not walk, and we had to carry him at a crouch through the sucking, sticky mud of the ditch towards the cover of the alleyway up ahead.

The assault team had cleared the buildings along either side of the alley, and at last we could rest. I was really feeling the strain. I had never been this tired. I was feeling sleepy and my legs were low on energy. I told myself to push one more step, and I was saying this to myself each step I was taking. I was thirsty, hungry, tired, hot, and did not know that the hardest test was ahead of us. On the other hand, I had kind of got used to hearing the bullets passing above our heads.

As we all rested our backs gratefully against the walls of the alleyway, the third and fourth groups came into the alley. Some were wounded, including another SFSG Para, who had been shot in the helmet, half an inch from the rim. He couldn't believe that his head had not been blown off, and was subjected to some teasing from the rest of the team. I shared my water and a few snacks I dug out from my pack, which were received gratefully.

I picked up the rifle of the wounded SAS guy on the stretcher. We would all have to take turns carrying him. I looked down the alley to the open space beyond and the slope of the valley's end beyond that. It had taken since before dawn under a blazing sun and constant fire to get to this point, but now we were close. We had only to run through a little square with a mosque at its corner, up a short alley, and the deadly flat, green, countryside would be behind us. Beyond it was a hill. It wasn't too steep but it was covered with sharp, unstable scree. Another problem was that this little square was probably the market place that the Taliban had marked out as the place where they could ambush us and finish us off.

The first team burst out into the square, through the little alley and started to climb the slope. Between them they were carrying the guy on the stretcher. Our hosts must have been taken by surprise. We watched the team run up the hill, slowing as they scrambled up the scree. I was listening to the Taliban radio, but they only spotted the group as it neared the top. I noticed that our guys slowed noticeably as they neared the brow, and at exactly the same time I heard an excited babble over the radio. Almost instantaneously they were pounded by heavy machine gun fire. Our medic was hit and wounded, but was helped over the skyline to safety.

By now the enemy was focused on the hill. The second team made its run. Again they cleared the little square without any bother. So much for the ambush. They came under intense fire going up the hill, but made use of a narrow gully to cover their run. Again I saw them slow agonizingly as they neared the top. They appeared to make it over the brow unscathed.

I was in the third team. The sergeant major turned to me and said, 'Eddie, I want you out of here. You're going first. Tell the APU guys the plan.' I passed on the information to them, and steeled myself for the ordeal. By this point I was not in good shape. The day had taken its toll. Thirst, hunger, walking for miles with full kit through a ditch with water up to my chest, all of it had degraded my body to jelly. Mentally I was becoming too exhausted to pay full attention to the Taliban chat, or send the correct messages to the Afghan Partner Unit, or talk to the detainees to try to get information out of them that would help us walk out of this place alive. On top of that I also had to be aware of my surroundings: the more eyes looking out for threats, the safer it was for us. Nothing, not even five-hour route marches through the desert in full kit, had prepared me for this level of exhaustion.

I looked at the sergeant major and he gave me the nod. I set off, bursting out from the cover and sprinting across the square. I was hardly half way across before I was fired on from the mosque. But before the shooter could zero in on me, an Apache helicopter roared overhead, strafing the mosque with machine-gun fire. The rest of the group sprinted behind me, with Sergeant Major Bob in the most dangerous place of all, bringing up the rear.

I gained the cover of the little alley, but didn't stop there. In a moment I was through, with the APU guys hard on my heels. I hit the slope keeping my head down. With every desperate fibre of my being, I willed my legs to drive me on up, but they answered with agony and fatigue. Every step took me into deeper scree. For every two steps up I took up the hill, I slipped back one, while bullets pinged around me, raking the loose pebbles. Each shot was getting closer.

'Get in the fucking gully, Eddie!' shouted the sergeant major from the back of the line. I looked back down and saw that the rest of them had ducked into the gully. In my desperation I had missed the entrance. I flung myself sideways, and pumped legs and arms across the rubble like a crab, rolling into cover with rounds kicking up the dust beside me. Without pausing, I picked myself up and ran at a crouch, shielded by the gully. I may not have been so exposed now, but the scree was just as deep and my legs were screaming with pain.

As I neared the top, the gully flattened out, and I realised why everyone else had slowed as if they were walking through tar.

The scree was deep, falling away in avalanches beneath my feet. I couldn't see how I was going to make it. Again the gunfire was getting closer. I would surely be hit at any moment. My legs were two bars of solid pain that were refusing to do what I asked them. All the while the chatter coming into both ears was providing a commentary on my own imminent death. Incredibly I made the last dozen or so yards without being hit, and threw myself to the ground, where the others who had made it so far were lying flat as bullets tore the air above us.

One by one the gasping APU men flopped down beside me, followed at last by Sergeant Major Bob. Even he looked slightly knackered. He clapped me on the shoulder and said, 'Bloody hell, Eddie! How did you miss the gully? I thought you were a goner!'

But our problems weren't over yet. The last group made it to the top, with Lieutenant Jones in the rear. He ordered us to stay where we were. We stayed there for half an hour, lying down as we couldn't stand or even kneel because of the incoming fire. I even had to pee lying down. The heat was almost unbearable – it was beating down and reflecting back from the rock and gravel. I found myself beside the injured Doc and gave him the last of my water. As for our prisoner, he was with the APU guys looking rather woebegone: not only had he had a hell of a day, but any hope of rescue was becoming a distant prospect.

We began to crawl away over the hill, dragging the injured man with us on his stretcher. Fairly soon we were on a downward slope on the other side and we could get up into a crouch.

As we collected ourselves, we started to contemplate the next task: another hill, higher than the first, and after that one more hill before the flat desert and the new evacuation point. But first we had to get away from the fire which was becoming heavier, if with decreasing accuracy as it became more indirect.

Over the radio I heard the Taliban chatterers discussing a suicide car packed with explosives which was coming for us. It did not get far before it was pulverised by a gunship.

Wearily we crept down the reverse slope to a place where there was enough cover for us to stand and up onto the next hill. Everyone took turns at carrying the two men on stretchers. Our bodies were so tired that nobody could carry them more than ten yards at a time before having to put the stretchers down and be relieved by another pair of aching hands.

By now it was about two o'clock in the afternoon. We walked for another hour before we came across a US medevac Chinook. The US medics relieved us of the wounded men. I asked one of them if they could give me some water. To my disappointment they refused: they were only here for the wounded. Then I remembered that I had a can of Red Bull in my pack somewhere. How could I have forgotten? I dug around until I unearthed the tin warmed by the day's heat. I opened it and sucked greedily at the hot, pink, sticky liquid. It tasted so rank that I threw the can away before I had finished, and carried on walking like a zombie towards the evacuation point another three miles away through baking desert.

At last we reached the waiting Chinooks. We stumbled wearily aboard one and were lifted out in a whirl of dust, happy that we had survived a horrible operation. My eyes kept looking at the coolers full of drink: water, Gatorades and a few other drinks. Luckily these American pilots were considerably more generous than their compatriots and the pilots started handing out ice-cold Gatorade and snacks. The drinks were passed onto each other very quickly and everyone was trying to down the bottles of drink at once. It felt amazing!

As we climbed, I looked back at the green valley. I couldn't believe how long it had taken us to travel the short distance from the local commander's compound. Soon the valley receded into a small, poisonous green slick in the dusty brown expanse of arid hills, and an hour later, at five o'clock in the afternoon, the Chinooks were touching down at Kandahar. It had been eighteen hours since we first got the intelligence intercept about our high grade prisoner, who was now walking mournfully under guard towards imprisonment, being given the odd propelling shove by the APU sergeant major.

I staggered out of the Chinook. My limbs had seized up in protest at the abuse they had received. I forced myself to take a shower to wash off the filth of the day and then crashed into bed about six o'clock, dazed and exhausted. I didn't wake up till late the following afternoon. When I came around, I thought for a brief moment that the previous day had been nothing more than a horrific nightmare. Then my aching muscles confirmed it was all true. Later I was given a medal for my part in this action.

Chapter 13

OC Terps – *Farmandeh Tarjuman ha*

Pretty soon I was put in charge of all interpreters. This was a validation, I like to think, of my honesty, intelligence and hard work. Many different people wanted to become interpreters. Firstly, the money was very good, and there were certainly some who did it for that alone. For those who came from very poor backgrounds, the salary on offer was a life-changing amount of money, no tax, free accommodation, free meal. An interpreter got paid enough in a month to feed a family of six for a several months. However, this wasn't the case for all interpreters.

One interpreter, Fahim, was a great guy from a very poor rural background. He was the only son, and his parents were expecting him to look after them in their old age. They debated long and hard about whether he should enlist as an interpreter. For an Afghan family, the oldest son of the family bears many responsibilities; he is literally retirement income for parents. He is also a godfather for the siblings and head of the family after the death of his father. Fahim was not just the oldest son, he was the only child of his family. There was no one else to look after his parents in their old age. In western countries, even in most Asian countries, when people get old, the state will usually look after them. Unfortunately due to poverty and incompetent leaders, Afghanistan has no such system. Instead the leaders of this country steal from the poor to feed their kids who live in mansions in Dubai.

Eventually they and he decided that the opportunity, though very risky, was too good to miss. He joined up to work for the US armed forces, not directly, but to work for a US army contractor who would take more than half of his salary as a commission to hire him. Within a month he was killed by an IED. He had not even received his first salary cheque. His parents were given $800 in compensation, but lost their beloved son and main breadwinner.

There were also interpreters who made fortunes out of their job – they became millionaires! And I am not talking millions in Afghani currency – I mean millions of US dollars. One interpreter in particular, in his early thirties now, landed contracts from Bagram air base which earned him millions in the matter of a year. I remember that by 2009 his ships were operating in the Arabian and Persian sea. Thousands of Afghans were employed by him to work on his projects around Afghanistan.

One of our interpreters, who was also working for our task force – we called him Jerry, a complete asshole – he was one of the interpreters who sympathized with the Taliban, who would treat the Taliban fighters arrested during operations better than his comrades. I could not get rid of him because it was the wish of one of the Afghan army officers to keep him there and he would speak very highly of him to our commanding officer during meetings. Jerry couldn't speak fluent English, and because of his dodgy nature I made sure he didn't attend meetings which were important or at which any classified material was discussed. During operations I always kept him with teams who were handling things which weren't particularly secret. He resented me for the way I treated terrorist Taliban, and also because I beat him in the fights we had during the time we worked together. He was one of those interpreters who joined NATO just for the money; there was no patriotism. He loved Pakistan more than Afghanistan. He would go on operations with us all night. We usually were back between 7 and 9 am and he would go for breakfast, take an hour nap, then drink Red Bull and in the heat of the southern Afghanistan summer would go and walk for hours, speaking to contacts whether they needed anything. I have to admit, as much as I disliked him for his ideology, I was impressed by his hard work. He had been a refugee: I guess one of the benefits of being a refugee child affected by war, it makes you strong mentally, it pushes your limits, the fear of poverty or going back to the bad times of refugee life motivates you to change your life by using every possibility. Where we were based, there were many US army contractors who were awarded contracts to build the bases. They could not go outside the wire to purchase materials needed for the projects, and this created opportunities for the interpreters or for the Afghans working in the bases. Jerry did this for a year or so and finally landed a contract to provide gravel for a company within the base. As soon as he was awarded this contract, he stopped showing up to work and so the team sacked him.

In our SAS team, there were between two and at times eight interpreters. Fortunately for us, with the SAS we did not lose any interpreters on operations. The SAS looked after us well. We were another member of the team. This encouraged interpreters to work honestly and loyally and we didn't mind being more than just interpreters. There were times when I was not only conducting operations from 6 pm to 9 am, but I also had responsibilities during the day. From my experience, British forces were fair when it came to justice: not only the SAS but the regular armed forces too were looked after well. Interpreters would eat the same food as British soldiers, live in similar accommodation, and wear the same protective equipment as any other British soldier. Stuff like that made us feel like another member of the team; even though we were local nationals, our service was recognized.

The Americans employed more than 5,000 interpreters at a time and at least five interpreters a week were killed – and those are only the ones I knew about. The main base for the Americans' interpreters was Camp Phoenix, in Kabul. That's where all the interpreters were hired and deployed to all over the country to serve with the US Armed forces. Their dead bodies would come back to the same camp. I am sure there were interpreters who got killed who I didn't hear about. The news of interpreters getting killed on operations wasn't worthy of broadcasting for the media. British forces also lost many interpreters, but the number was never acknowledged. I know one interpreter for the British forces who lost two legs and one hand. Hundreds of other interpreters lost body parts as well. Those interpreters have all been left behind or were let down.

ISAF troops and units were rotated out as their tours ended, going to their own countries for leave or assigned to other duties. Interpreters had their own leave depending on their job and responsibility. Some couldn't go home more than once a year due to lack of secure transport going to their homes, and sometimes they had to wait a year or so for the army to arrange a seat for them to travel on a convoy. They could not get any R&R immediately after their ISAF unit's handover, as they had to help show the new team around and introduce them to their counterparts. In my case, I had to give my brief about Afghan Partner Unit officers. I had to tell them whether they were good or not, and how to interact with them to achieve our goals. It wasn't easy to work with Afghan officers: their mood would change more often and quickly than the English weather. The unit that we were dealing with, it was like talking to a bunch of kids with attention-seeking issues.

Some interpreters joined for the same reasons I did: the excitement and the desire to effect positive change for their country, to serve people of a nation who had suffered for decades from terrorism, extremism and regional politics.

Others, although a low number, joined to spy on the British and Americans for the Taliban or the Pakistani security services. We came across various types of these characters, and I used various ways to weed them out of our corps of interpreters.

On one occasion I had to interrogate a Taliban fighter when the Afghan Judicial Officer instructed me not to translate everything for the SAS. He also told the Taliban fighter he did not have to tell the British everything. He started to feed the prisoner a story. Clearly he thought that I should, as an Afghan, be on his side – or he did not care. I protested about him to the British officer in the room and he was removed, but I was not the only one who could see his actions on the field, the SAS also kept an eye on him during operations. This ambivalence was common amongst some Afghan government people and ANA soldiers. Those officers who were Pashtun felt bad to see their fellow Pashtuns getting arrested, even though the very same Pashtun 'brother' would happily kill them and their families given half a reason to; in fact Pashtuns are the ones who have suffered the most from the terrorism they breed.

Even Afghans inimical to the Taliban could feel resentful about the interpreters. They called us 'Afghan infidels'. Our high rates of pay earned us resentment from nearly all ranks of the Afghan National Army, police and other officials with whom we were supposed to cooperate closely. My salary was better than that of a brigadier. They also resented the fact that I would not pass on intelligence I gathered for the British army to them. But as far as I was concerned, I was working for the British forces: it was a question of duty. More importantly, I wouldn't trust them with any intelligence unless they were cleared, but unfortunately Afghan forces did not have a credible system of vetting their recruits; almost anyone could join, and the results were seen later during the increase in 'green on blue' attacks. Many Afghan national army soldiers who were loyal to the Taliban attacked and killed many NATO forces.

Interpreters had an extraordinary role and responsibility in the battle for Afghanistan. We had a unique opportunity to evaluate all sides in the conflict, and often had a special insight into when a battle was fought well and when it failed. The role of the interpreter was so much more varied than mere translation that it is not an exaggeration to say that we played a significant role shaping modern Afghanistan. It was us who stood in the middle between all the parties, domestic and international, who fought to contain and defeat the Taliban. Yet interpreters' efforts were never recognized and the real number of interpreters killed in action was never revealed. Interpreters are the forgotten heroes who played a significant role in the war against terrorism.

Chapter 14

Operation Prison Break – *Musa Qala*

I have conducted hundreds of special operations over the years in Afghanistan. All of them saved lives of innocent people, in particular Afghan people. Such operations just motivated me further, to take part in more operations. They also brought a chance to hear people appreciate what we did. Not many appreciated our work. Most believed we just operated at night and killed kids. More people believed the Taliban's propaganda than the facts on the ground.

Usually our operations room would work on a number of targets, so until the last minute we had no idea what target we would be hitting that night. It all depended on the urgency of the operation, how big a threat it was, and some other factors.

That night was to be a prison break, to free people who were in the Taliban's captivity, people who had been tortured for weeks and were being executed on a daily basis. I did not know that we would be going for this target; I simply stopped what I was doing and hurried to get to the briefing on time. It was around 9 pm and all we were told was that we had to get prepared for a mission, nothing else.

When we were prepared and waiting in our operation room, the squadron officer in command and sergeant major gave us our orders, which were to break into a prison and free the prisoners.

We were excited. On the way to the target all I was thinking about was how happy the prisoners would be once we had freed them from the Taliban. I could only imagine what it would be like to be a prisoner of the terrorist Taliban's prisoners, whose only justice was their barbaric interpretation of Islamic law.

We got to our target, and as we landed, a few hundred metres away from the targeted compound, we heard some shots coming from our left. At this stage our assault team was way ahead of us. I and others were in a different Chinook and we landed a bit further away. As we were approaching the prison, we were told on the radio from the ops room that they could see movement within the prison and that one of the targets was running towards the river (which was right next to the prison).

The group that was moving towards us from the left was engaged by our aircraft and were burned so badly that they smelled like kebab! In fact I thought that some crazy Afghan must have been hungry and was making kebab at this time. I could smell them for days after the operation – the bastards ruined kebab for me! As we were walking towards the compound, I saw two terrorists still burning. It was difficult to work out their structure. All I could see was their heads and bodies; their hands and at least one leg were missing. It was a good motivational scene: seeing them get what they deserved was very pleasing.

As soon as we got close to the prison, the Taliban guards started shooting at us, but our assault team, who was closer to them, shot them down. They then moved into the compound room where they killed the remaining terrorists who were resisting there. As usual they were well armed, with plenty of ammunition.

After all the Taliban members who resisted had been killed, I was asked to move to the breach point, which was the other side of the compound, where the prisoners were held. I called for everyone to come out with their hands up, so we could identify if they were Taliban or prisoner. The assault team did not assault this part of the compound; the important thing was to get the prisoners out in one piece.

As the first person came out of the prison, I could see he was chained: his hands, legs and one round his neck. He was obviously a prisoner and I told my Sergeant Major (SGM) so. As he was approaching us, another person came out, running towards the other side of the compound. He was a Taliban guard hiding with the prisoners. We shot him down and he was killed there.

After clearing the prison, we found that there were thirty-four prisoners and much evidence which led to successful future operations.

Before taking them back to base with us to free them, we had to interrogate them to be sure we were taking only the legitimate prisoners, not the Taliban. After several hours with the prisoners, we found out that one Taliban was hiding amongst them. These guys were still very afraid after what they had been through, and they feared that if they gave up the one Taliban member, he would come back and kill either them or their families. It was a very long time until even one of them spoke up. The Taliban was pretending to be the prisoner who suffered the most. The way he was answering my questions was unbelievably deceptive.

We interrogated them once more, to make sure there was no error, and then I chatted with them informally. They could not stop smiling all this time and could not wait to go to their families. They told me that they had all accepted their fate and that this would be their last few days. They saw their fellow prisoners being executed daily, based on the judgment of a mullah from Pakistan, and they had no hope but to wait for their time.

They had all been living in one room, approximately 5m x 4m, with one window, and were all sleeping on the floor. They had to ask their families to bring food for them, as the Taliban would not provide for them but instead were taking money from their families. They were not allowed to take a shower or have phones and had to remain in chains in their room. Almost all said that they had been tortured daily. A couple of them had injuries that looked a few days old, and our medic helped them out. Later they were treated in a British camp in Helmand.

Among these prisoners there were soldiers from the army, police officers, Afghan government employees, and a few who had been arrested for not having beards or some other nonsense reason. Joyful and happy as they were, each had a story to tell. The story I found most fascinating was that when we conducted this operation it was Ramadan, which means the month of fasting for the Muslim world, and they break their fast in the evening or the end of that day. Before breaking their fast, they all gather to pray, to wish for something, and these prisoners told me that they all prayed that this prison would be raided tonight. I think someone out there heard their prayers and sent us to free them.

After separating them, the officer in command decided to evacuate the prisoners and take them to the closest base, hand them over to the local authority to help them, and then release them.

In the end it was a victory for the local politicians, who took full credit even though those politicians had no idea of the operation until the morning after we entered the base.

Chapter 15

Afghan Infidel – *Kafera Watani*

The end game for the British army, and ISAF in general, was to set up a viable Afghan state, with strong institutions. And the most important institution they needed to create was a strong and functioning Afghan National Defence and Security Force or ANDSF. This chapter will describe the part I played in the attempt to set up an Afghan special forces unit.

The British government poured huge amounts of money into this project, and the Afghan National Police special forces received a lot of meticulous training from the SAS and SBS. However, the unit was riven by ethnic tensions between the officers and men. Recruits were taken on through patronage rather than rigorous selection courses. Although this unit was more successful than others, thanks to the sacrifices of the UK special forces, there was another unit, a new special forces unit in the south, which was an absolute nightmare to deal with.

One senior officer was raking off $50,000 a month from pay supposed to go the unit's soldiers. When his nephew, a squadron leader in the unit, blew the whistle on his corrupt uncle, he had to go into hiding, eventually taking refuge in the UK where he lives to this day. He did it because his uncle wouldn't share the stolen money from the food of the soldiers with him.

I was loathed by the corrupt officers of the unit, who were making a killing from diverting funds meant to train and supply the men. It was about now that I realised that the biggest threat to me was going to be the Afghans on my own side, who I thought were the future of Afghanistan. Supposedly these men were the most anti-Taliban, anti-terrorist forces in Afghanistan. Maybe I was being naïve, but I wanted an Afghanistan where there was no institutional corruption. It was this reason, more than my duty to the British army, that made me take a stand.

I crossed an ANDSF officer who tried to tell me not to translate certain things for the SAS, and to pass on information to him instead. I not only told him where to get off, but got him sacked.

The death threats to me and my family from the ANDSF, rather than the Taliban, finally convinced me that we had to leave the country. The news of NATO withdrawal increased the urgency to leave even more. It not only encouraged Taliban, but delighted the corrupt who were in power, who would in future be able to act with impunity.

Eventually the rotten unit performed so badly and was so riddled with corruption that it became a source of embarrassment to the ANP. It would have been disbanded if it had not been for one of the first recruits of this unit, a Sandhurst graduate, Khushal Sadaat. When he got into power he saved his unit by not only bringing a pro-Afghan and anti-Taliban ideology, but also reforms.

The SAS, through unofficial channels, laid the foundations for a much-improved SF unit with a proper *esprit de corps* and selection process. It has been successful, particularly in taking back the city of Kunduz from the Taliban, and at the time of writing was still fighting effectively in Helmand province.

Chapter 16

Extraction – *Faraar*

Eventually my outspokenness and refusal to betray my employers in the British army made me too many enemies in the Afghan establishment. The ANDSF incident was not the only one where I had reason to fear the Afghans on my own side more than the Taliban. In another, the Taliban claimed that the SAS had shot an innocent man. I had witnessed the incident, which happened during an operation. An insurgent had tried to use his own son as protection from being shot, waving the toddler in front of him. The SAS skillfully dropped the man and saved the child. We took photos of the dead man, who was wearing his chest rig, and cleared the area. The next day, however, the Taliban put a photograph of the dead man on the internet claiming he had been unarmed – they had removed his weapon and chest rig. The SAS vehemently denied this version of events and produced their own photos. The incident became a *cause célèbre*, attracting the attention of President Karzai, who launched an inquiry into the matter, to which I was invited with delegations from the police, the ANA and units from other forces. I refused to go. I had a strong suspicion that I would be 'disappeared' if I went anywhere near the president's office. This and other incidents like it made me very unpopular with my compatriots high up in the government and the ANA.

The Taliban often changed the scene and claimed that the insurgents killed were innocent civilians; in fact they used this tactic after almost every special operation. The challenge was that the special forces community could not share their evidence as they did not want to reveal their methodology, so almost every time, the judgement of public opinion went against them, and some of the naïve Afghan media and the media of the West would buy the story.

After the Kajaki incident, which is still circulating on the UK media, my life changed. The threats I was receiving became too dangerous and real. At the moment this was coming to a head, I was asked to go to the UK to help train soldiers about to go on tour in Afghanistan. Just after I got my visa I realised how serious things were getting when I heard that the APU were threatening to shoot me on campus. Previously on many occasions after operations their soldiers would warn me that they would shoot me when they got a chance, and I would ignore these cowards' threats. But later they were determined to get rid of me. One day I got a call from the officer commanding the APU who said, 'You know that you have a family outside the base. Your father, your mother and your brother. You do know that these forces will not be there to protect you. Eventually they will have to leave.' It was clear what he was insinuating. That was when I really got scared. Before, I felt safe on campus, as there were plenty of US and British troops about. But I knew at that moment that I would have to leave the country I love. Worse, I knew that my whole family would have to leave as well – not just my parents, brothers and sisters, but all of my relatives. This had no good outcome.

Still it took me some time to make up my mind. As a former interpreter for the US army I was entitled to US citizenship under a programme initiated by George Bush. But I did not want to go to America. I did not want to go the UK either – I wanted to stay and serve the people of Afghanistan. Then the day before I was due to leave, another APU guy came up to me and said: 'The British won't be around forever. One day they will leave, then you know that taking a life in Afghanistan isn't as difficult.' Another warning.

A few days later, I flew to Camp Bastion to wait for the plane to get us out of the country. While we were waiting we went to the chow hall to eat food prepared for the passengers by the British army. By the time it was my turn, all that was left was a few ham sandwiches. For me eating ham or beef really doesn't make any difference, but there was an Afghan officer on the same flight and when he saw me eating pork sandwiches he said, 'I'll make sure you account for that when you get back.' I ignored him. I like pork sandwiches.

We waited three days in the stifling heat of Helmand. Finally we were told that we were leaving next. We boarded the plane, it took off, on the plane we were offered drinks, and I ordered a beer. The same Afghan officer leaned over and said, 'You know, you drink alcohol, you eat pork, you're not really a Muslim.' Then he launched into a lecture. I cut him short. 'Look. I don't really care about your opinion. You do what you want, let me do what I want.' I could see the hatred in his heart. I was becoming more and more sure about my decision not to come back. What surprised and pissed me off at the same time was that a few minutes later he ordered a beer and just looked at me with a smile. I was angry to see this hypocrisy: You cannot drink, you should be killed for drinking, but I can and its okay. That was their logic. So really eating pork, drinking, and anything else, all was an excuse – they were hiding the real reasons they resented me. Instead of having another useless lecture with him I just told him to enjoy it. I enjoyed my beer and started a conversation with the passenger next to me, a British officer, with whom I had a much more meaningful conversation.

We were supposed to go to Brize Norton but landed at Heathrow. I was surprised not to be searched. The SAS officer and I had some coffee, and then I was taken in a car to the training area. I was there for two nights, but as far as the training went, I was not in the right mood. It was meant to be as realistic as possible. The set-up included some Afghans who were now UK citizens playing the part of villagers. My nerves were so jangly that I treated them like insurgents! I was doing my usual job showing the soldiers how it was done, but I was aggressive and loud. All the army boys appreciated it, but the people who were acting as villagers were not happy. I suppose it was good training in a way, as the interpreters who were there had never seen it done before. It was counted a success, a really good exercise. I felt bad for the way exercises were being handled in the UK. The British soldiers were not very realistic, the actors or role-players were not even close to what they would face in Afghanistan.

Afterwards I was taken to various places for more briefings and exercises. The last stop was in central London. By now I had decided for sure that I couldn't go back. The SAS guys I was with back in Afghanistan anticipated that I would not return. In the run up to my departure they would say, 'Are you really going to come back?' I always said, 'Yeah, sure I am,' and I meant what I said. But some of the people I knew and was close with would reply, 'Don't. Honestly mate, don't.' I think they would have been disappointed if I returned. We all knew I was a marked man.

The threats I faced were not only verbal: on three occasions I was physically attacked right in front of the SAS. If it was not for the SAS NCOs who saved me, I would have been killed in Helmand, in the early months of 2011.

On one occasion, I was interrogating a terrorist on the targeted compound. My method of interrogation was different, something the APU or the Afghan special forces did not agree to. As I finished my interrogation, I was talking to the sergeant major about the intel I had received from the terrorist. The APU officer who was guarding the door probably heard me during my interrogation of the terrorist, and he came to me, grabbed me by the neck, pointed his pistol at me with his other hand and threatened to kill me. But immediately, the SAS sergeant major pushed him and warned him of the consequences if he put his hands on me again.

I still had to find out what to do and who to see. I had seven days left on my visa to stay in the UK. I negotiated the London tube system for the first time and found my way to Croydon, a piece of navigation of which I felt rather proud. All the way there I had a feeling in my gut that I could not describe: something like hope and loss at the same time. Not just the loss of my country, but of my job, which I loved. The hope was less definable, as I really didn't know how my life would go from now.

I went into the Croydon Immigration and Asylum Support Service and asked for an interview. They asked me to wait while they brought an interpreter, even though I was speaking English to them. I said, 'Look I'm not going to speak to you through an interpreter. I can speak English.' After the interpreter had gone they asked me how long I had been here. I replied to the lady who was sitting behind a glass screen.

'Five days.'

'I don't believe you.' She replied with a judgmental face.

'Look here's my visa. I've still got a week left on it.'

'No you must have been here longer than that. You're lying.'

Because I spoke English so fluently, they simply wouldn't believe that I hadn't been here illegally for a very long time. That's when I told her that I had been an interpreter for the British forces. She told me to go back to the seats and sit there as I would be called back again in due course.

At this point two policemen came in and arrested me. They took me to a different room and searched me. They even put me in handcuffs.

'Look,' I protested, 'Here's my visa! Call the Ministry of Defence, call the army. They'll tell you who I am.'

'Don't worry, we will,' they replied as I was hauled off to the detention centre.

After a few hours of wait, I was told that my case would be fast-tracked. They would investigate it quickly and then decide to either send me back or allow me to stay. I was detained and then I was taken to Wandsworth Prison. They put me into a cell with a Sri Lankan, an ex-Tamil Tiger fighter who had escaped Sri Lanka and execution. He escaped his death but not the nightmares which kept him and me awake all night. The room was just another typical prison cell: a small TV, a toilet and a bunk bed for two. I took the bottom bed and the Sri Lankan the top. It was a proper prison: they locked the doors at 10 pm and everyone had to go to sleep, and then opened it at 7 am for everyone to take a shower and then eat.

I was disappointed with the way they treated me. I did not deserve it, after serving the British army to my best. I was loyal and my loyalty cost me everything, almost got me killed, and yet I was treated just like an illegal immigrant. I do not regret working loyally for my employers… but I was disappointed.

I was told to stay there for the weekend and that I would have an interview on Monday. So I thought that in the meantime I would talk to these guys who were locked in with me and hear their stories.

The following day, Monday, I was interviewed by a Home Office official, who was more worried about me revealing secrets than the decision he would make about my life.

'Before we start, I know who you are and who you worked for. Please don't tell me anything which will result in the SAS chasing me. I do not want them to come after me. If you can't answer a question, please let me know and I will not ask again,' he said to me with a nervous smile on his face.

I assured him that I would not share anything sensitive with him regardless. I was here for my case, and my story had nothing to do with the details of what we were doing in Afghanistan.

After a few questions, he decided to let me live in a different part of the prison, which allowed me to have my phone and walk outside or play cricket. I felt free and hopeful of walking out, which happened the day after. The day my next battle started.

Chapter 17

A Second Front – *Jang e dowoom*

I laboured under a delusion when I came to the UK that the Afghans who had emigrated here would be the most enlightened of all Afghans, as they would have escaped the ignorance and prejudice of home. By living abroad, they would have absorbed the best that the wider world, and in particular the west, would have to offer. They would be wise, progressive and tolerant.

Two days in detention shredded that belief.

In the detention centre I thought that I could speak freely – I was in the United Kingdom of Great Britain! Some other Afghans at the facility asked me what I did for a living in Afghanistan, and I told them happily, 'I was working for NATO.' They were outraged and started shouting at me that I was a traitor to my country. They hated Britain and told me I was the worst kind of infidel. I was dumbfounded. I felt like I was in Kajaki, speaking to members of the Taliban who had seen nowhere but Kajaki.

'And you guys are trying to claim asylum here?' I asked in disbelief.

'You know,' said one of them menacingly, 'if I ever catch you in Afghanistan, or even here if I can get away with it, I will hang you by the tongue for what you did.'

I was stunned. To begin with I believed that maybe these Afghans were being deported, but I soon realised that this attitude was endemic. Some of the detainees couldn't speak English. I asked them how they could want to come to a country they hated, even though they knew nothing of the UK and its culture. One had no idea where Wales was: he thought it must be another country, somewhere in Europe. They believed that Britain was what they had learned it to be in their closed, small communities; they believed in myths; rumours rather than facts. To me it seemed deeply wrong. When you go to another country you accept its rules. I had absolutely nothing in common with these people. Most fantasized of an Afghanistan under the Taliban. But they were hypocrites: they wanted those rules for others but not for themselves; they wanted Halal. This mentality was mostly among the Pashtun communities of the eastern provinces of Afghanistan. They are more loyal to Pakistan than to their own country.

On the second day I was given another interview, what they call a screening interview. This interviewer was also nervous.

'I know who you are,' he said, 'I don't want you to tell me anything about your missions, or anything else that could be classified. I really don't want the army after me.'

'All I can tell you is what I'm allowed to tell you anyway. I am here about seeking asylum. Details of operations have nothing to do with it,' I replied.

He proceeded to tell me that there was a complication with my application. Later I learned that the APU had complained to the FCO and the task force commander, making a lot of false claims that I had to go back because there were allegations of murder against me by one of the Afghan judicial officers. They tried to use the case of the alleged SAS murder of an unarmed Afghan against me.

But the British government knew who I was, and they knew these charges were false. The APU did their best – they sent an official letter. They even went to my parents, saying 'You need to get him back here.'

At the Home Office I told the truth: 'I don't have anything to hide. I am here for a genuine reason and that's the truth. You can confirm it with the MOD.'

Shortly afterwards I was accepted into the asylum process, but I was told by someone from the Home Office who met me at the detention centre that I was not going to be fast-tracked. I was driven to Glasgow in a rather curious manner. First I was taken to a service station near Birmingham, then swapped into another car and taken to Manchester, and then into another car to Glasgow. When I got there I was shocked by the cold: 'Oh my God it's freezing!' I thought to myself.

I was put into a depressing block for asylum seekers. After that I was moved to a flat near Easterhouse where I had a ten o'clock curfew, and then to another flat in the area that I shared with a succession of asylum-seeker flatmates. It was not exactly the warmest of welcomes, but I soon discovered that the locals were friendly, even if some were pretty rough.

One of the guys who briefly shared my flat was an Afghan who told me that his cousin had spent some time in Glasgow and then later claimed asylum as an interpreter. They gave him his paperwork immediately. I was disappointed by that, particularly as he had a strong Glaswegian accent and his English was terrible. I don't know how he got away with it.

The same guy introduced me to others in Glasgow's Afghan community. One of them asked me to join the Scottish Afghan Society – or SAS as it was called, ironically. Their ignorance was shocking. They hated each other. They hated Tajiks, and any other Afghan who wasn't Pashtun. The Scottish Afghan Society was only for Pashtuns of that city, though weirdly it was a Tajik who encouraged me to join. If other Afghans tried to join them, they were discouraged. I met several of them. They carried so much hatred and expressed such extremism. They were the worst Afghans I have ever met. Despite this, the Scottish Afghan Society is supposed to be the official Afghan society in Glasgow, and receives government funding.

I wanted nothing to do with them. I told a few of them that I had been an interpreter for NATO in Afghanistan and it drove them insane with rage.

I would say to them, 'Why are you here then? Just go back if you really believe that.'

One of them said, 'Our women were safe back then [under the Taliban].'

'OK,' I would reply, 'If the Taliban told your women to wear a burka and that's so great, then why aren't they wearing a burka here? They ordered all men not to shave, so why are you shaved?'

It made no difference: they bore their ignorance like a badge of honour and believed only Taliban propaganda. If I told them how things really were, they refused to have a discussion.

I asked them about the mosque they were building, for which they got funding from the government. 'They are helping you build a mosque. If you hate them why do you use their money?'

'It's good to use their money, but not good to follow their rules.'

'But that makes you like the bad guys, like thieves!'

They asked me what I was going to do here, and I told them that my plan was to enter into education and get some qualifications. They scoffed at this, 'You don't need an education. We can get you a job within the community. The British aren't your friends, and they will not employ you. We can give you jobs in our shops. You will be better off within the community.'

What they meant by the community was the Muslim community. This comprised mostly Pakistanis, Bangladeshis and Afghans. It was pretty clear that they just wanted me to be cheap labour. I never met any of these guys who was anything more than a taxi driver, delivery man, pizza chef or shop floor sweeper. All of which is fine if that's the limit of your ambition, but it was not for me. I wondered how many new arrivals had been closed behind the community's doors, shackled to dead-end jobs, exploited by these so-called community leaders. I met some poor souls who had been here for sixteen years or more and couldn't speak English.

I knew the direction I wanted to take, and I avoided them. I don't think they were that bothered, particularly after I told them that I was Afghan first and Muslim second.

'No, no! Don't be like that! You are a Muslim first, Afghan second!'

'Sorry, mate. Afghanistan is my religion. That's it.'

I lived in Glasgow for about nine months. My family had moved to India with my parents – they weren't to join me till just before Christmas 2013. During that time I went to London quite a lot, seeing guys I had worked with. They were doing their utmost to help me, talking to MPs and other influential people. I appeared in an article in *The Times*, on the strength of which a very good solicitor took my case on a voluntary basis. But still the Home Office was dragging its feet over my asylum application. I decided to write them a letter, encouraged by my new solicitor. When I look at that letter now, I see how desperate I was. I had fallen into a limbo where I couldn't work, couldn't get an education, couldn't progress. I said in it that if working for the SAS was wrong, what was right? I was really tired of the process.

Thanks to the letter and my solicitor, they speeded up the process from months to a few days. I finally got my papers through. The feeling of relief was incredible.

A former boss of mine got me a job in Ledbury working for an agricultural company, as well as finding me a flat in this beautiful town. It was a great job in many ways, and I was delighted to be earning money again at last. However, in the end my heart wasn't in it.

I moved to London, but after spending a year in London, I realized that London was not the city for me and I moved to a different city close to London. There I worked as an interpreter for the council, social services, the NHS and the police. I mostly interpreted for Afghans and Pakistanis. I saw some terrible cases, involving domestic violence, rape, child abuse, drug dealing and smuggling. But there were also mundane things like speeding tickets. The funny thing about Afghans is that when in Afghanistan they don't want their women to talk to anyone; in England, however, their women are allowed to talk to any other men, any other nationality, except Afghan men. So when I was translating for women who were visiting the doctor, I first had to translate what the doctor said to the husband, for him to repeat the same thing to his wife, who was sitting next to him; and then whatever his wife said, the husband had to repeat it to me, then I would say it in English to the doctor. Unbelievable! Taliban ideology all over again. Some are even worse than Taliban. I wouldn't have done it if it hadn't been for the money.

On a separate assignment, I was translating for an Afghan woman who had been here for only a few weeks. Her father-in-law was with her. The nurse asked her if she was happy, to which she replied, 'No' (in Pashtu). Before I could speak, her father said, 'You can't say that in front of them, or you will suffer when we get home.' I told the nurse immediately what was going on, but there was little they could do.

In Afghanistan, many girls are forced to marry guys three times older than they are. They are forced to do things they don't want to, they are raped and they are abused. For some, when they get out of the country, it's an opportunity to break free, but unfortunately, for those who have families in Afghanistan, they continue to be oppressed even after leaving the country.

In some cities it is common practice for the council to send new asylum seekers and immigrants to the local mosque if they are Muslim, and especially if they are Pakistani, Afghan or Bangladeshi. I was sometimes called in to interpret for these youths, who were all male between their late teens and mid-twenties.

I was annoyed that these young men, some of them not much older than children, were being packed off to the mosque and fostered by Muslim families, without any choice on their part.

One day two kids were being interviewed by the council and were told that they were going to be sent to the local mosque, to get introduced to the Imam. As soon as I translated this to the boys, they looked uneasy and looked at each other, fear in their faces. I intervened and said, 'Are you going to send them if they don't want to go?' The council officer looked completely non-plussed and asked, 'Do you think they might not want to go?'

'Well they don't look particularly happy about it do they?'

So he asked them if they wanted to go to the mosque. The two boys looked very uncertain. I then had to explain to the council officer that he would have to explain the idea of freedom of choice to them: where they came from it was simply not an option to say you didn't want to go to the mosque.

Eventually the two of us got this across to the boys, that they had free will. They could go where they wanted, they didn't have to go to the mosque, or live within the Muslim community. At first they couldn't believe us. Then when it sunk in, they decided happily that they would rather not go to the mosque.

They were fostered by a non-Muslim English family; they learnt English in about six months and are doing well. It was a great lesson for the council: the boys were very happy with their family and very happy with the progress they were making and the friends they had.

On another occasion a Pakistani boy was showing reluctance to be fostered by a Pakistani family. The foster father and the council persuaded him that it would be in his best interests, especially when the father said he would be educated in his own language. Not long afterwards the boy came back complaining that far from being educated in his own language he was being forced to learn Arabic in a private madrassa, and wasn't being taught English at all. This foster family, who had looked after dozens of kids, were constantly the focus of complaints from their charges for the way they abused them, mainly by forcing them to learn Arabic and not feeding them enough, despite the large amounts of money they received from the council. This boy was moved to another family.

So many of these kids disappear into a ghetto where they are taught to fear and hate British society and are prey to the teachings of deeply prejudiced imams. When the council went to the local mosque, reputed locally as moderate, to discuss the wider implications of this, the very first thing the mullah said was, 'Of course we all hate you. You're bombing our countries!' There was no question of debate.

In my view this wilful withdrawal from British society is the biggest problem facing Muslim communities in Britain. It is often reinforced by the fact that imams are nearly always recruited from Pakistan or any other Arab country, and are woefully backward, and deeply prejudiced against Britain and the west. I remember talking to an imam in Helmand once when I was on patrol. I asked him how he was qualified to be an imam. He said because his father had been one, and the local people just came to him for religious instruction. I asked him what sort of qualification was that? He replied stiffly that he had been to a madrassa in Pakistan to train. I asked him if he could read. No, he replied, but he had learnt the Quran by heart. This was typical of many mullahs. They can read the Quran, which is in Arabic, but they have no clue of the meaning. Although the Arabic alphabet is similar to Farsi and Pashtu, this mullah was not able to read or write. The only book he read was the Quran, with the interpretation made up by senior Taliban, tailored to benefit their propaganda.

This ghetto mentality reinforces group paranoia. Why do Afghans put up with it? I know plenty of Iranians and they don't behave like this. I haven't come across any Iranian ghettos. They manage to integrate and take full advantage of the opportunity that Britain offers without losing their national identity. The same goes for Indonesians. So it isn't just a matter of being Muslim.

But it is depressing, and it is dangerous. In a way I have merely been continuing the war my father fought for progress and enlightenment. I will never take the existence of this ghetto mentality as a given. I will always confront it, to try to shake people out of their apathy, to make them think beyond their self-imposed prison. They are denying their children the opportunities that this country has to offer. I would like Afghanistan to have the same freedoms and advantages as the west. I would like my country to break the shackles of religion and tradition and join the best of the modern world; to make things rather than just take them.

The worst of it is that many in Britain encourage this terrible abuse in the name of multiculturalism, or for some long-forgotten colonial guilt. They aren't doing anyone any favours, and are allowing yet another generation to have their minds warped because they don't know any better, to become fodder for the extremists' crazy war.

*   *   *

Thanks to the death threats of the ANA, my family are now scattered to the four corners of the world. The people who drag down Afghanistan with corruption are just the other side of the Taliban coin. One day I pray that Afghanistan will have strong and honest institutions and can become a nation once again. I also hope that Britain won't betray its Muslim community, and its other citizens, by allowing the breeding grounds of ignorance to foster the next generation of jihadists.

I will always regret the fact that my military career is over. Those were the best days of my life. It was my calling. Now all I have left is the inevitable PTSD that comes from prolonged exposure to warfare. I have nightmares, and I know that they will be with me forever.

I am not the only one suffering from PTSD, and certainly there are many who have it worse than me. I have spoken about it to people I served with, some of them soldiers. They have given me differing advice: 'Don't allow it to take control of you,' they say. 'Do the opposite of what it is telling you to do.'

Recently I have been studying at university, and have been learning about PTSD as part of my degree. It is hard to concentrate. When lecturers talk about it and how it affects the brain, it helps me understand, even though they talk about cases that aren't as serious as mine. I am as aware of it as you would be of a physical injury. I cannot discuss my own situation with my lecturers because I can't discuss my previous work. I know that if I could find someone to talk to who knows or is allowed to know about these operations I would get better. I don't see anyone about it professionally: if you can't talk about everything to a psychologist, then as far as I can see there isn't much point in seeing one. At the moment I am doing my best to fight it by keeping my job, education and contact with family.

Recently I have worked with refugees who have PTSD. For me, it has been good and bad. On the positive side I have learnt about how to cope with it, how it is treated, and I use that information for myself. On the negative side it reminds me of my nightmares.

Since I first came here, a slow change has come over me. To begin with all I wanted to do was to return to Afghanistan, to make a difference, maybe in politics. But that dream is fading.

I am a 35-year-old man, suffering from PTSD, I am hated by many Afghans and others, and I can probably never visit my country again. I have many traumatic memories that stretch from childhood to only a few years ago, that will haunt me for a long time. Many of my friends ask me if I regret what I did. Was it worth it? If I could, would I do it all over again? I do not regret a thing. Sure, there are some things that I would do differently, but when it comes to my job, I did what I did for the cause I believe in strongly. If I went back in time and was asked to do the same job all over again, I would do it again and count whatever I lost along the way as worth it for that cause. It was my dream to fight for a free Afghanistan, and I lived my dream. No-one's life is perfect. What we do always has consequences, but I have already faced them and looked them in the eye. I am prepared for whatever comes next. I am prepared to continue fighting for what I believe in one way or another. Only this time, I want to fight Islamic extremism in the United Kingdom.